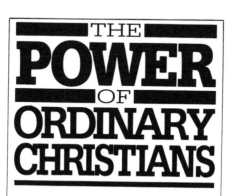

MARGARET WOLD

THE POWER OF ORDINARY CHRISTIANS

Witnessing in Jesus' Name

AUGSBURG Publishing House • Minneapolis

THE POWER OF ORDINARY CHRISTIANS
Witnessing in Jesus' Name

Scripture quotations unless otherwise noted are from the Holy Bible: New International Version. Copyright 1978 by the New York International Bible Society. Used by permission of Zondervan Bible Publishers.

Scripture quotations marked TEV are from The Good News Bible, Today's English Version, copyright 1966, 1971, 1976 by American Bible Society. Used by permission.

Scripture quotations marked RSV are from the Revised Standard Version of the Bible, copyright 1946, 1952, and 1971 by the Division of Christian Education of the National Council of Churches.

Library of Congress Cataloging-in-Publication Data

Wold, Marge.
    THE POWER OF ORDINARY CHRISTIANS.

    1. Christian life—1960–   . 2. Witness bearing
(Christianity) I. Title.
BV4501.2.W578   1988   248'.5   88-10507
ISBN 0-8066-2374-8

Manufactured in the U.S.A.   APH 10-5036

  2   3   4   5   6   7   8   9   0   1   2   3   4   5   6   7   8   9

CONTENTS

PREFACE

A few dozen ordinary people, armed only with words, wine, and bread, brought hope back into a world from which the promises of God seemed to have retreated. In the power of the Holy Spirit, they witnessed to what they had seen and heard in Jesus and they changed their world. This book is about today's ordinary Christians who have the same power for witness and for change. The need for us all to use this power is urgent. Our lives depend on it!

1

PARABLE
OF A SEEKER

Our book begins with a parable about a secret passage, a seeker, and a dark closet with a locked door.

When our son, Erling Jr., was 10 years of age we lived in a big, beautiful old house in North Dakota. Ten big rooms on three floors, a full basement, lots of closets, hallways, and surprising nooks and crannies made it an inviting place to live after years of one-story, basementless and attic-less California ranch-style homes.

A neighbor who loved to spin tales told us the history of that house was one of mystery and intrigue.

"The story goes," he elaborated on a visit to welcome us to the neighborhood, "that it was built by a bootlegger during the days of prohibition." Obviously relishing his tale, our neighbor went on, "The story goes that this bootlegger built a secret passageway somewhere in the house that leads to an underground tunnel that he had dug clear through the backyard and under the river way over to the other bank on the Minnesota side! Then, just in case the federal agents raided his house, he could escape to another state where he had another hideaway."

My husband and I laughed at this tale, but our son's youthful imagination was fired by the story. Then, one day while vacuuming, when we uncovered a pushbutton under the carpeting on the steps leading to the third floor, our son was sure the story was based on fact. What else could a hidden button be for but to open a secret trapdoor somewhere? We explained that it was no doubt a call button for a housekeeper or servant who lived in the third floor apartment.

Erling Jr. preferred to think otherwise.

One wintry Saturday afternoon I asked him if he wanted to go to the grocery store with me or to stay at home alone.

He'd rather stay home, he said.

I left him with the usual motherly instructions about keeping the doors locked and not to snack too much, and promised to be back as soon as I could.

Erling Jr., left alone in the empty house with Saturday afternoon at his disposal, decided that this was the time to find the secret passageway.

Flashlight in hand, he climbed a stairway going up from the kitchen to the third floor. He planned to work his way down to the basement after thoroughly examining each one of the upper stories.

Finding nothing promising on the third floor, he came down to the second where four bedrooms, a sun porch, and lots of closets and storage places held more promise.

One large closet invited him. He walked in, his flashlight probing the secrets of the dark, windowless storeroom. As he pushed aside the still unpacked assorted boxes and bags he was unaware that the door was swinging shut behind him until he heard it slam and lock.

Swinging around he saw in the beam of the flashlight that there was no knob on the inside of the door!

He was helplessly trapped in a small room without windows and with a door that could only be opened by someone else on the outside.

Alone in the closet, Erling was all right until the battery in his light burned out. In the dark, fear grabbed him. The frightful situation woke all of the primitive fears that sleep under our healthy, waking hours waiting for such dark moments to surface and torment us.

I came home, wondered where he was and called for him. I soon heard his muffled cries, ran upstairs, opened the door and released a desperate but jubilant boy from his dark prison.

The explosive good news

The true meaning of our parable is that shattering explosion of love and joy that burst from the grave with Jesus Christ!

With the resurrection of Jesus Christ from the dead, a locked door was opened in human experience and all of our human options were changed.

We who are caught in our human dilemmas, trapped by our own histories and decisions, bound by our desires and cravings, tied to our sins and the inevitable decay of our bodies, tormented by our memories and misdeeds, we now have an alternative to despair!

"I have come that they may have life, and have it to the full" (John 10:10) was the promise Jesus gave to his disciples before his enemies killed him on a Roman cross.

Death seemed to have triumphed over life.

But the good news is that death did *not* have the final answer.

Life with a capital "L" is our option right now, while we are still alive!

Are we too sophisticated, we modern folk, to believe such a simple gospel? Has the "new physics" of which we hear so much replaced God as a system of belief? Now that we know all about our decaying entropic universe, can the resurrection of Jesus Christ speak in quite the same way to dying humans as it spoke in the past?

Or does the book of Ecclesiastes become the only valid way of looking at life when it describes everything we are and do as "meaningless, a chasing after the wind" (1:14)?

The wise but cynical author, identified as the great King Solomon, sighs at the end of his life, "Yet when I surveyed all that my hands had done and what I had toiled to achieve, everything was meaningless, a chasing after the wind; nothing was gained under the sun" (2:11).

Weary of the world and facing death, his only advice is to eat, drink, and be merry in this earthly existence because "All share a common destiny—the righteous and the wicked, the good and the bad, the clean and the unclean. . . . The same destiny overtakes all. The hearts of men, moreover, are full of evil and there is madness in their hearts while they live, and afterward they join the dead" (9:2,3).

The New Testament affirms that we have reason to despair. "The wages of sin is death," the apostle Paul wrote to the church in Rome (6:23), and we are all "dead in . . . transgressions and sins," in which we used to live (Eph. 2:1,2). This death traps us in our locked closets, and we are helpless to move out of our dyings. We become those "who all their lives were held in slavery by their fear of death" (Heb. 2:15).

A cover story on the frightening AIDS epidemic in *Newsweek* magazine (Aug. 10, 1987) related the poignant cries of some who have lost their lives to the dreadful disease.

"Come closer," a 26-year-old pleaded, dying. "I'm afraid."

Another, younger, mourned, "I'm not afraid of dying, I'm afraid of being alone."

To people trapped by sure death, the resurrection of Jesus has been the only piece of good news ever to speak to this universal condition.

The resurrection reveals God as the source of hope in a dying world and as the source of love for a people depressed by an existence seemingly devoid of meaning and plagued by unabsolved guilts and the fear of a dark and lonely death.

Laurence Olivier, the late great British actor, said in an interview a couple of years before his death, "The worst part of me—the most boring part—is my guilt complex. I feel almost responsible for the fall of Adam and Eve. . . . Once you have those feelings, they don't go away. It (his wife's illness) was my fault, of course. Everything is, what isn't? Now that I've admitted it, I'm looking for a little absolution" (*People,* Jan. 10, 1983).

What about ordinary women and men who move through life in a progression of routine days? Do they feel trapped? Does the thought of death and abandonment bother them? Do they worry about guilt?

I'm aware that I may be projecting my own guilt feelings and fears onto the rest of humankind. But I think theologian Dr. Joseph Sittler summed up what Olivier and the rest of us are feeling guilty about when he affirmed in his book *Gravity and Grace* (Augsburg, 1986) that "the facts of life (including my own life) as I look at them—the betrayals, the forgetfulness, the selfishness, the egocentricity—are but the history of humankind written small."

If we could only share our feelings, talk about our fears, we would undoubtedly discover that we share them in their primitive form with most other humans.

When a friend of mine was participating in a study of grief that was being carried out by the sociology department of a large university, she was required to call on people who had lost to death a spouse, parent, or child within the past two years.

A significant part of her findings was the surprise most people she interviewed exhibited over the fact that anyone wanted to talk to them about their experience. Generally friends and relatives and acquaintances had avoided the topic even though the bereaved person was hungry for someone with whom to share feelings and memories.

Underneath so much of our reluctance to face death as a fact of life and our unwillingness to talk about it is the unbearable feeling of loneliness aroused in us by such thoughts.

With great insight and honesty, the young man dying of AIDS had confessed, "I'm not afraid of dying. I'm afraid of being alone."

That's what it's all about, isn't it? That's what Dr. Karen Horney called our "basic anxiety." It is the fear of abandonment, of being alone in a friendless world, and, ultimately, alone in a godless eternity.

To avoid the pain of that anxiety, we avoid anxiety-producing subjects. The problem with this pain-avoidance behavior is that we never can talk about hope and healing for the pain.

Wise Dr. Sittler sharply reminded us that "we must stop this conspiracy of silence about death, and talk openly about it. One can go to church a whole lifetime and never hear a sermon on death."

Reminiscing, he reminded us, "If I were a young preacher again, I would preach the Christian gospel of eternal life in God, but I would preach it more realistically. The Bible really has nothing to say about eternal life. That sounds like a shocking statement, but it's literally true: there is not a single clear and concrete word in the Bible about life after death. It affirms that life with God is life with that which does not die" *(Gravity and Grace)*.

If Erling Jr. had had a friend in the closet with him, being locked in would have been an adventure; alone, it was for him a dreadful, not soon forgotten nightmare.

Life with God, as Sittler said, is just that—"life with that which does not die." It is life with Someone, made possible because we have been set free from the bondage of death by the action of Jesus Christ in human history.

What a contrast to Albert Camus' lonely "stranger," the character in his novel *The Stranger* who, emptied of hope, sees, instead of the creating, redeeming, loving God, only "the benign indifference of the universe." He thought that in order "to feel less lonely, all that remained to hope" for was the possibility that on the day of his execution for a pointless murder, thoughtlessly committed, that "there should be a huge crowd of spectators and that they should greet" him with "howls of execration."

Even a jeering, cursing mob was preferable to dying all alone, especially for this man who denied the existence of God.

The exhilarating good news proclaimed by the empty tomb is that light has come into all of our dark places, that locked doors of fear and loneliness are opened, that, instead of the "benign indifference of the universe" we have been put in touch with a God who is personal and available.

Of all this no "proof" exists beyond the words of the Book—the Bible—the evidence of human history, and the testimonies of countless millions all over the globe who have discovered its truth in their own experience.

We're not expected to *prove* the gospel; just to offer our witness to it as an option to despair and hopelessness, a possible opening of some locked doors, the potential release of some captives.

After freedom, what?

Being released from the closet brought immediate joy and relief to our son. Later on came some bad dreams, moments of unexpected panic, some phobias, all of which had to be brought under the joy of the moment of release. That happy moment and its emotion had to address all of his later experiences.

The death from which Jesus releases us brings resurrection power to all of those little deaths through which we pass in a lifetime.

When the psalmist wrote, "Even though I walk through the valley of the shadow of death, I will fear no evil, for you are with me . . ." I wonder if he was referring to all of life? Doesn't the shadow of death hang over all of life from birth onward?

More important than the release from the closet, then, is the walk we take after we're set free. How do we make it day by day, hour by hour, minute by minute? How do we survive the small terrors, the second-long panics, the wandering fears that come when we least expect them?

"You are with me. . . ."

When one participates in the resurrected life, the presence of Jesus, the resurrected one, transforms everything.

Richard Eder wrote in the *Los Angeles Times* (Aug. 2, 1987) of his first experience, as a young reporter, of seeing a corpse—a young man shot dead in a New York subway by the police. Afterward, wrote Eder, he remembered riding the subway home in the early morning and noticing that "what normally seemed scruffy—grimy cars, a drunk or two—suddenly shone. Simply because they were alive, or served life."

That sense of newness of life is an essential part of the good news! "The old has gone, the new has come" wrote Paul, the transformed Saul (1 Cor. 5:17).

A student once asked a Bible teacher whether or not Jesus ever laughed. The teacher said he didn't know, but "one thing I do know is that he changed me so that I can laugh!" The living presence of Jesus makes the difference.

"Surely I will be with you always . . ." (Matt. 28:20).

Traveling in Europe with my brother when he was a foreign service officer with the U.S. State Department was a particularly enjoyable experience. When he showed his diplomatic passport at various checkpoints, we would be waved on our way without any further questions. His official presence imparted immunity from interrogation for all who were in his party. Although I had a valid passport and had nothing to worry about, I felt much more secure when I was with him.

The saga of seeking goes on

We've had the good news around for thousands of years. Yet, the quest for a new world, for security from fear and for assurance of immortality still lures people into the futile search for another gospel.

What are we looking for that God has not already provided in Jesus Christ?

In August of 1987 the announcement was made public that, on a certain weekend in that month, electrical vibrations arriving from outer space would resonate through the earth and galaxy to usher humanity into a new age. People were urged to look into ancient Mayan and Aztec calendars for revelations validating this prediction. Five "sacred" places around the globe were identified as points of "harmonic convergence."

The hopeful gathered at these places. Nothing happened to change the flow of daily bad news.

A young woman named Nancy interpreted her experience at one of these sites. "A lot of people gathered together Sunday morning to see something very beautiful," she said. "But it happens every morning. The sun rose" (the *Los Angeles Times,* Aug. 17, 1987).

One expert in mythologies, John Lash, gave his explanation for these kinds of perennial phenomena. "People are needy. They periodically sense—especially toward the end of a century—a millenium, that it requires a power greater than themselves to bring about that which they desire. They become vulnerable, susceptible" (the *Los Angeles Times,* Aug. 12, 1987).

The neediness of people for new beginnings, for some security in the face of an unpredictable future, and for answers to the meanings of life and death will always create vulnerability to new ideologies.

Exactly this neediness was evident in the Graeco-Roman world into which Jesus was born. The apostle Paul makes reference to the spiritual hunger of that world when he points, in Acts 17:23, to many "objects of your worship" that he observed as he spoke to the Athenians about Jesus and his resurrection.

The poignancy of their longings reveals itself in his words to them, "I even found an altar with this inscription: TO AN UNKNOWN GOD."

That period in human history was the appropriate time—the Scripture reads "the time had fully come" (Gal. 4:4)—for the plan of God "which he purposed in Christ" (Eph. 1:9) to be carried out.

The interest in reincarnation, cosmic vibrations, in occult powers, and in things like harmonic convergence, are evidence that a vast need still exists for our witness to the fact that the new age *has already come* in Jesus Christ.

God has promised that those who seek will find what they are seeking. They may follow wrong directions, and they may stumble into blind alleys and dead-end streets. They may get themselves trapped in seemingly hopeless situations but, if their longing is for the living God, the promise of Scripture is that they will find what they are looking for.

Although salvation belongs to God in Christ, the mission of God has been entrusted to people living in God's world who have experienced new life in Christ.

Human ears must listen for human cries, human tongues must speak the words that set people free, human feet must run swiftly to release the captives, and human hands must be quick to open locked doors.

Christians cannot abdicate their responsibility for a continuing witness when they know that the search for hidden secrets will continue, often to the peril of those who are being led into situations that endanger their bodies, minds, and spirits.

Into the neediness of people on the quest for newness of life, we bring our witness to the new Life in Jesus Christ.

That is our privilege and our responsibility.

2

IS ANYBODY LISTENING?

Walking down the hill to the mailbox one day, I met our neighbor coming back up. Ours was a typical California neighbor relationship, based simply on such chance encounters. A couple of days before he had mentioned that his wife was not feeling well so I stopped him to inquire about her.

"The lab report came back showing something abnormal in her liver," he said. "We won't find out about the bone scan for a week. But it doesn't look good."

"I'm sorry," I said.

He went on. "I've been through this so many times. I've seen my mother, a sister, and other members of both of our families die of cancer. I don't know if I can go through something like that again."

We stood in the morning sunlight, birds chirping cheerily in the trees around us and bees buzzing busily in some blossoming bushes nearby, while he poured out his fears and pain. Tears filled his eyes and brought a tremor to his voice.

Finally, unable to continue, he reached out and squeezed my arm and walked on up the hill.

I called after him. "If you ever want to talk about it, come on over."

A familiar scenario

Do you recognize the script? Anyone who reads this book could have written it. Who hasn't had neighbors who need a listening ear when their lives seem to be falling apart?

Our worlds are full of people with a story to tell and no one to listen. My husband Erling and I have been the guest leaders at many retreats where we have stayed up half the night listening to such stories.

Example. You've been a passenger on a plane. You greet the person sitting next to you and that simple word of greeting becomes, to your surprise, an invitation for your seatmate to tell you his or her personal history. You never do get that book read that you had looked forward to reading on the plane!

I remember Cliff. It was Sunday morning and I was on my way to speak at a church service in San Francisco. I couldn't help but be aware of the nice-looking man sitting in my row in the aisle seat. The flight attendants seemed to know him and kept coming by to chat and to offer him coffee.

Since the plane was scheduled to arrive just in time for someone to pick me up at the airport and whisk me over to the church, I felt that I had to use the hour-long flight for some last minute preparation.

If you ever open a Bible on a plane you can be quite certain that someone will respond one way or another to that action! Out of the corner of my eye, I could see the other passenger looking at me.

Soon he leaned over and asked, "What are you reading?"

"Well, I have to speak at a church in a little while and I'm studying the Bible passage that I'm using as the basis for my talk this morning." I smiled and went back to my reading, hoping that this was not going to be one of those times when a chatty fellow passenger would keep me from getting anything done.

He stuck out his hand and introduced himself. "My name is Cliff and I'm very interested in knowing what you're going to talk about."

So I told him I was going to speak about Ezekiel 37, the Bible text listed in the church lectionary for that Sunday and, sighing inaudibly, I began to close the Bible as I sensed I was being drawn into a conversation.

"Do you mind reading it to me?" Cliff asked to my surprise.

Wondering about his interest, I read him the story of Ezekiel's magnificent vision of the valley of dry bones, uneasily aware that this ancient story was probably most inappropriate for the handsome, well-groomed man who, I thought, appeared to be a stereotypical, successful businessman.

When I finished, Cliff sat reflecting and then he said, quite simply, "You have just read the story of my life."

I laid my Bible and notes aside and listened as he described his own private "valley of dry bones."

He painted a tragic picture of his months and years as a combat helicopter pilot in Vietnam, of his after-the-war angers and frustrations and bouts of wife-battering, of his divorce and the denial of visiting rights with his children, of his experiments with drugs and his descent into despair, and of the ultimate loss of his airline job.

When he was finished, I realized that my sermon was being written for me.

The final paragraphs of Cliff's story could be entitled, "How the Dry Bones of My Life Became Muscles and Sinew and Skin and Danced in the Valley," as he described the resurrection that had recently come to him through the concern of another pilot who told him about God's love in Jesus Christ.

The new "confessional"

Give the least little sign that you're open to listening and the world's warehouse of woes will pour its contents into your ears.

If everybody has a story to tell, who's going to do the listening? Who's going to say the words of absolution and of hope that were once only available from a priest?

Counseling grew significantly as a profession after the Protestant Reformation when the church confessional diminished in importance.

We're not talking about persons who need psychotherapy, or who may be suffering from severe neuroses or be psychotic, but we're talking about the person next door, on the plane, on the bus, in one's office. The person who just needs "someone to talk to."

Moving the confessional out of the church placed it in the marketplace, squarely in the middle of the mainstream of life.

Now the confessional is anywhere and everywhere.

"Confess your sins to each other and pray for each other so that you may be healed," wrote James, the brother of Jesus (5:16). How easily one can substitute a host of other words for the word *sin!* Words like *illnesses, pains, heartaches, fears,* all of the human conditions that call for healing.

Whatever is wounded in a person's life can be translated into a story that's seeking a listener and, if possible, a healer.

Listening creates the walls of a confessional into which the speaker can enter with confidence. Through the person of the human listener, Jesus Christ the great high priest can move in to accomplish his healing action.

Compassionate listening

Compassion creates the climate in which healing can take place.

What an elegant word! *Compassion.*

A good word for God.

"O God . . . according to your great compassion blot out my transgressions" (Ps. 51:1).

"The Lord is full of compassion and mercy . . ." (James 5:11).

Jesus "had compassion on them and healed their sick" (Matt. 14:14).

Jesus said "I have compassion for these people; they . . . have nothing to eat" (Matt. 15:32).

"And when the Lord saw her, he had compassion on her. . . . And he said, 'Young man, I say to you, arise.' And the dead man sat up. . . . And he gave him to his mother" (Luke 7:13-15 RSV).

Jesus "had compassion on them, because they were like sheep without a shepherd. So he began teaching them many things" (Mark 6:34).

Forgiveness, mercy, healing, feeding, giving new life, teaching the uninformed—all of these actions are compassionate.

More than pity, sympathy, or empathy—the feelings that accompany compassion—the ordinary Christian who is compassionate transmits an energy that works to accomplish what is needed in the life of another person.

When the compassionate person *listens,* one knows that the listening will result in active response.

When the sinned-against, oppressed, abused person, the stranger, the widow, the orphan, the poor, cries out to God, the promise is "I will hear, for I am compassionate" (Exod. 22:27). The listening, hearing God will not let the wrong go without a responsive action!

Compassionate listening exhausts the hearer, calling forth all of the spiritual, intellectual, and physical resources she or he has available.

All the while one is listening to the speaker, one is also listening to that small, inner voice of the Spirit counseling, helping, guiding, giving ideas, offering solutions, pouring strength into one's being.

The Spirit whispers, "Don't judge; just love and do whatever love demands. Be forgiving. Love this person as you love yourself, remember? What do you think is behind the words? Enter into the story, imagine yourself in it. What's really happening? Is there a wrong that needs righting?"

Compassion makes us practitioners of love.

The Spirit sketches the face and form of the dying and risen Jesus in bold relief on our hearts and compassion transfers his image onto the face and form of the one to whom we are listening.

Compassion turns abstract, theological love into active loving.

Practicing compassionate listening

The ability to be heard depends on the willingness and the capacity of others to listen. Watch someone whom you consider a good listener. How does that person's body reflect good listening? What is there that indicates total absorption in another's story?

First of all, you will probably notice the listener's eyes. Ears don't reveal much about listening, but eyes do. The eyes of the good listener are focused on the other person's face, most likely they are locked into the storyteller's eyes.

Can you stay focused on another person's eyes? Or do you find yourself easily distracted by peripheral movements? Often our own emotional stability is reflected in our ability to maintain continuous eye contact with another person.

Nothing speaks more loudly to the other person about our concern for their story than our eyes. If they continually drift to other people or objects in the environment, that says very clearly that we really aren't interested. Whatever we speak after that won't make much of an impact on the one whom our eyes have rejected.

Secondly, our body language speaks of our interest or disinterest in the speaker.

The good listener will be relaxed and waiting but will be leaning, in an easy manner, slightly toward the speaker. What effect does it have on you when you're talking to someone and she or he leans back in the chair and locks hands behind his or her head?

What if someone starts tapping the desk with her pencil, or starts cleaning his nails? How do you feel if she closes her eyes? Or if you see his eyes looking stealthily at his watch or the wall clock? Or at a magazine lying nearby?

The good listener responds appropriately and honestly. If your mind wandered, don't be afraid to say so.

If the story becomes repetitious, rather than revealing disinterest by means of covert actions, you can perhaps lead the speaker in a new direction with a suggestion like, "I need to hear more about your feelings when that happens." Then again, the repetition may be a clue to the nature of the concern.

If time is a factor, tell that to the speaker and make an appointment to meet at another time.

My posture on the plane was certainly not designed to encourage Cliff to speak to me. My actions gave a clear signal, "Don't bother me!"

Cliff had to overcome a lot of resistance to get me to listen to his story. Unlike the Samaritan of Jesus' story, I was not moved by compassion to listen to his pain, much less to bind up his wounds. "Which of these . . . was a neighbor to the man?" (Luke 10:33-37).

In fact, which one of us was the "listener" and which the "speaker"?

I was not open to listening because I didn't want to give up my own agenda. Cliff's persistence forced me to listen. Then I thought that I was being asked by the Spirit to be a witness to Cliff. Instead, the roles were reversed. Cliff's story became a witness to me.

Cliff taught me something that day about persistence.

If you think you have a word of good news to share, persist and share it. Although I was feeling annoyed by his interruption of my study time, I was glad he had overcome my reluctance to engage in conversation with him.

Lately, there's been much in the press about a lifestyle called "cocooning." People are making their homes into "cocoons" in which they can shield themselves from the world and all of its problems, its brutal violences, and its enormous dilemmas. Home gymnasiums, home video recorders and movies, soft couches, entertainment centers, pools, spas, and security systems make the cocoon invincible. One is reminded of the medieval castles with fortresslike walls and guard towers and their drawbridged moats!

Only the wealthy can afford to be totally cocooned. But many of us indulge in psychological and emotional cocooning. Obviously, I was even using my Bible as a shield against intruders on the plane that Sunday morning.

Perhaps you use church activities as a way of cocooning yourself. Bible classes, prayer meetings, musical groups that fill every day of the week can effectively cut off all communication with people who are looking for a compassionate listener and someone who can bring them a word of hope.

We ordinary Christians need to make ourselves available, approachable, and touchable, and to plan opportunities for listening to those who need to talk.

Being a good listener does not make one a therapist or qualify one to give advice or to make life-changing decisions for another person but it does qualify one to present one's own witness to the newness Jesus Christ has brought into one's life.

Speak to me!

The Gbaya people of west central Africa greet one another with the all-purpose word *wurmo*. Literally translated, it means "speak to me" or "say something."

Like our "How are you?" this word can be quite frustrating to the foreigner who is taught to use it in greeting but then has no more words to say in response!

The Gbayas are sociable people and do not like to have anyone left out of a conversation. If they are gathered together and one person is not participating in the conversation, one of them will turn to that person with a warm smile and say "Wurmo!"

With that word they acknowledge the person's presence as if to say, "Yes, friend, we know you're here and want you to know that we haven't forgotten about you. Join us if you want to."

They offer what every human encounter promises, an exchange of gifts and of words that open one's heart to the other person's very being.

Eventually, then, in any listening situation one must respond to the other person's story with words of one's own.

In our speaking, through our Spirit-empowered witness, Jesus Christ the Word Incarnate takes shape and becomes flesh through the spoken words.

Spoken words were all there was in those early decades after Jesus' death and resurrection. Just spoken words for at least 20 years afterward. People *told* other people what they had seen Jesus do and what they heard him say when he lived among them. There were no tracts or New Testament writings to pass around.

Of course they had the written Hebrew and Greek Old Testament, but the word about Jesus came from first-hand experience and it was in their hearts, in their heads, and in their mouths, and they had to *speak* it in order for it to have life and the power to make Jesus come alive for others!

One of those "witnesses," a disciple named John, wrote later on to tell others how it all got started. "That which was from the beginning," he wrote, "which we have heard, which we have seen with our eyes, which we have looked at and our hands have touched—this we proclaim, concerning the Word of life. The life appeared; we have seen it, and testify to it, and we proclaim to you the eternal life which was with the Father and has appeared to us. We proclaim to you what we have seen and heard" (1 John 1:1-3).

"Wurmo!"—"speak to me" says the Gbaya.

And we say that to each other.

When it's time to say something

The time comes when you can no longer remain silent. The "nondirective" type of listening may be fine for counselors, but it is only part of the context for the Christian witness.

After the story has been told and you have cared and listened, then the Word must become flesh through you and your flesh must become the Word for others.

Words, poor as they may be for communicating eternal truths, are all we have. A popular song captures that when it sings, "Words, words are all I've got. . . ."

People rely on the power of the spoken word.

How much more meaningful the words are when we can see the love in the eyes of the one who speaks them and hear the quality of tenderness and compassion in the voice! Words on the printed page are available to be pondered and studied, but on the lips of a living witness they take on added meaning.

At Stratford-upon-Avon we saw a performance of Shakespeare's play *Twelfth Night.* In preparation for our visit to the theatre we read a copy of the play.

We agreed that the plot, characters, and lines did not seem particularly impressive. In fact, not having read or seen the play before, I wondered if it was really worth seeing.

Then we saw the play.

What a difference! Through the voices and the actions of the actors, the play came alive, the lines seemed brilliant, the plot inspired, the characterizations subtle and many-faceted.

Some of this respect and appreciation for the spoken, living words may have inspired the third chapter of Paul's second letter to the church in Corinth. "You yourselves are our letter," he wrote, "written on our hearts, known and read by everybody. . . . You show that you are a letter from Christ, the result of our ministry, written . . . not on tablets of stone but on tablets of human hearts" (3:2-3).

Written words are often used in a legalistic fashion to prove dogmas and to win theological arguments, but when we give our witness to Jesus the Word Incarnate, it proves nothing except that we have seen, heard, touched, and been touched by the resurrected Lord Jesus Christ. Paul put it quite bluntly when he wrote, "for the letter kills, but the Spirit gives life" (2 Cor. 3:6).

Thank God that we have the written Bible as the witness of those who walked and talked with the Lord but unless they come to life through us they cannot be available to most of the world's population.

The ideal understanding of the importance of our oral witness may have been articulated by the prophet Jeremiah, who wrote, "Then the Lord reached out his hand and touched my mouth and said to me, 'Now, I have put my words in your mouth' " (1:9).

The early followers of Jesus were in no hurry to write the words down. The Lord had come and put the Word in their mouths.

Of course in those days they believed that Jesus was coming back in his promised "second coming" right away. "I tell you the truth" he had said to them, "some who are standing here will not taste death before they see the kingdom of God come with power" (Mark 9:1).

The gospel as kerygma

Even when some of them died there seemed to be no rush to put the *kerygma* into written form. (*Kerygma* is a noun form from the Greek verb meaning "to proclaim as a herald" or "to announce."

The disciples were to make oral proclamation, *kerygma*, of the good news about Jesus Christ: that he had been sent by God to fulfill the times, that he had carried on a ministry validated by all of the "signs and wonders" associated with the Messiah, that he had died an unjust death but one that was God's will, that he had been raised from the dead, that he was now seated at the right hand of God, that he would come back to carry out the final judgment and consummation of all things and he would usher in the ultimate reign of God.

This was the message the apostle Peter declared (Acts 2:22-36). When people heard the *kerygma*, they believed.

To this objective proclamation of the historical realities of Jesus' life and death, the apostle Paul added the story of his own experience of the living Lord Jesus who appeared to him on the road one day and changed the direction of Paul's life, dramatically and conclusively (Acts 9:1-9).

Paul never forgot his life-changing experience and he talked freely and openly about it, adding it to his proclamation of Jesus' mission and message.

When we speak our own *kerygma*, it must contain both of these elements, the objective facts of the good news that Jesus brought to the world and the subjective experience of that good news in our own lives.

The power of the Word in any contemporary situation was recalled on the 40th anniversary of the founding of the Lutheran World Federation. Quoting from a message at the First Assembly, the speaker said,

> From those who have languished in prison cells, in dungeons, and behind barbed-wire barricades, came the cry: 'Back to the Bible.' They have discovered the Old Testament as the Word of God in very truth. They have learned to know the apostles of the New Testament as their own contemporaries, as they have faced the evil in the hearts of men, and as they have witnessed the power of God to save.
>
> (*The Lutheran Standard,* Aug. 7, 1987)

What happened 2000 years ago when Jesus lived in the small country of Palestine must come alive in the lives of people today.

Does the story you tell, the word you speak, make sense when it encounters the stories to which you are a listener?

Out of your own experience with the good news of Jesus Christ do you have a good news *kerygma* of your own to speak to your neighbor?

Conversion

The goal of our listening and speaking, what we hope to have happen, is a change in the life of both the listener and the speaker. We are seeking some kind of "conversion," a change from darkness to light, from the power of Satan to the kingdom of God, from the despair of sin and death to the joy of new life in Christ.

We're on touchy ground here. The word *conversion* sounds simple-minded to many modern sophisticates.

It conjures up pictures of "fanatics" who have lost touch with reality, of followers of secret cults and strange sects.

Martin Luther abhorred people who were what he called "enthusiasts" who let their emotional experience become a substitute for the freely given grace of God, grace which operates on our behalf independent of any actions or emotional responses on our part.

Emotional reactions and feelings come and go but faith as a gift of God is based only on what Jesus has done on our behalf.

For Luther the great change in his life came as a result of his encounter with the grace of God in the words of Paul's letter to the Romans, "For in (the gospel) a righteousness from God is revealed, a righteousness that is by faith from first to last, just as it is written: 'The righteous shall live by faith' " (1:17).

The chains that had bound Luther's spirit broke away, the dread of God's wrath that had driven him to physical self-torture and spiritual agony was replaced by freedom, joy, and the desire to tell everyone else about his new understanding.

For Luther, this was a conversion experience, the gift of God that turned him from the bondage of despair to the wholeness of salvation in Christ with all of the joy and fullness of life that goes with it.

The seed planted in his spirit in Baptism bore the fruit it was destined to bear. Paul did not know when he gave his witness to the church at Rome that a man named Luther would some day read his words, have his spirit renewed and his thinking transformed and become, in his own right, a powerful witness for Christ.

Neither do we, when we listen to the pains of others and are led by the Spirit to share our own *kerygma*, neither do we know what fruit it will bear in the lives of those we touch, but our prayer and aim is that through it, Christ may be "formed" in those others (Gal. 4:19).

Listen, then! What do you hear?

Do you hear the cries of men and women and children to whom no one is listening?

Will you listen and speak?

The *kerygma* is written in the Word and is waiting to become flesh through you.

3

ORDINARY CHRISTIANS

We went to church in Africa this spring.

The church in Africa

Mud brick walls and an aluminum roof formed a shelter for perhaps 300 worshipers. The pews were plank benches and the floor was hard-packed red dirt. We walked there on dusty dirt roads under a burning sun to join the lines of people converging from every direction on that unadorned house of worship.

The Africans came, crowding into the church until there was standing room only.

Women came, brightening the plain sanctuary in their brightly patterned shirts, wraparound skirts, and headcoverings. Babies were there, too, tied on their mothers' backs, carried in their arms, nursing at their breasts, toddling by their sides, or still developing in their bodies.

Men in clean white shirts and slacks walked and sat with their older sons.

With the people came joy and laughter and singing. Coming together, the gathering itself, was a lilting litany of worship.

We, with our white, uncolored skin and plain, Western clothing, felt alien to that vivid fellowship. That feeling did not stay with us very long since we were soon caught up in the most exhilarating worship time in which we'd ever been involved.

Even before we entered the crowded doorway, hands were extended to us, smiles welcomed us, the Gbaya greeting, "Wurmo!" and the French "ça va!" swept us along into the fellowship of African Christians.

The service followed a more or less traditional liturgy so that, even though the language was unfamiliar to us, we felt included by the familiar cadences and responses.

But the singing and the spirit of total joy in worship was something we had never experienced before!

The words of the hymns were approximately the same as in English, we were told later, but the music was strictly African. The beat of several kinds of homemade percussion instruments and the rhythms of a variety of sticks, tambourines, and sand or gravel filled cans and boxes tied us all together in one living organism with their common pulsebeat.

The choirs, three of them, came in one at a time before the service began, each with its own unique style, instruments, and rhythms.

Before the actual service began, at least half an hour was given over to the choirs. The congregation joined in the singing whenever people were moved to do so.

It seemed to us that the choirs were all trying to outdo one another in giving praise to God! The congregation that morning was a living reenactment of Psalm 150, paraphrased,

Praise the Lord!
Praise God in the sanctuary! . . .
Praise God with trumpet sound!
Praise God with lute and harp!
Praise God with timbrel and dance!
Praise God with strings and pipe!
Praise God with sounding cymbals! . . .
Let everything that breathes praise
the Lord!
Praise the Lord!

There was dancing. Not the wild, uncontrolled frenzied sensuality of cultic dancing, but the deliberate, rhythmic swaying of bodies caught up in a wholistic worship experience.

The worshipers "danced" into the church, they danced up to the altar with their offering, they danced as they sang in the choirs and in the pews.

The church in England

Three months later we were studying in Oxford and we went to church in some of the great cathedrals of England. The contrast between the two cultures, both of which we experienced in that short period of time, could not have been more profound.

Since that time we have found ourselves pondering the differences, especially in worship styles, in both places.

It may be totally unfair to compare the two but the comparisons keep coming to mind. I could just as well be comparing the African church to the American church since England and the United States are part of the same Western world.

The church in England is so much older than anything we have in the United States. A thousand-year-old cathedral has no rival in our country. If a church building is one hundred years old, it's considered a historic monument here.

Africa is the same in that respect. Mud brick churches do not last a long time nor does wood in termite-infested African countries. The church can always start over in Africa while in England the monumental structures determine the ongoing life of the church.

Our question

The question that keeps coming up in our discussions time and again is this one: Why is the Protestant church in Africa growing so vigorously in numbers and in worship attendance while the same churches in Western countries are dwindling in numbers and attendance at worship?

Aware that this same question has captured the attention of wiser and more experienced heads than ours and aware that a brief visit to Africa and England does not make us experts on those places, we are forced by our fresh, first-time observations to share our reflections.

The role of the laity

In Africa, the church is a church of vigorous lay leadership and participation. Professional clergy do not dominate the Protestant Churches in Africa. Professional leadership is as scarce as it was in the New Testament and when it is present its role is one of support for the nonprofessionals as the "people of God."

Our invitation to participate in the life of the church in the Central African Republic and the Republic of Cameroon had come from the Association of Evangelical Lutheran Church Missionaries. We were asked by them to speak at their annual retreat for spiritual renewal, following a visit to the places where they all lived and worked.

While there, they told us that the churches in their countries were completely under the leadership of the African people now and even the missionaries were there only at the invitation of the indigenous church.

No longer did missionaries serve as pastors of congregations there. They came as teachers, principals, doctors, nurses, mechanics, engineers, linguists, and agriculturalists to supplement and support the work of the local church among its people.

When the missionaries pulled back from direct church leadership positions and allowed the people to control their own church life, the church in Africa experienced new growth.

The people began to take ownership of their own church life.

African lay evangelists and catechists do most of the work of outreach among the people. They provide for the needs of their families through their own efforts at gardening and other occupations just as the early disciples did. The rest of their time and energy is devoted to their real vocation of teaching and bringing in new converts.

Pastors serve in a local congregation but also have some supervisory responsibilities for the congregations where lay people are in charge most of the time.

Lay people do most of the preaching and all of the teaching in most of the local congregations.

By contrast, the church in the West, represented for us by our worship experiences in England, is controlled by professionals. The preaching is done by clergymen, the choirs are composed of highly trained musicians who sing music of much technical difficulty. In fact most of the famed choirs only use male voices.

All of the worship leaders wore vestments of some kind, a practice which further separates leadership from laity.

The order of service is highly structured, allowing only for very controlled lay participation through responsive readings and structured body movements—sitting, standing, kneeling on cue. Clapping, musical instruments in the hands of the lay members, freedom of movement, and nonprofessional choirs are not allowed.

One might argue that this sort of worship is best suited to the British people until one considers the fact that only three percent of the people in England go to church on a Sunday morning and are active in other ways in the church.

Active laity, growing church

If the gospel is to make any impact in our world today it will happen through the combined influence of every one of us individual Christians right where we live day in and day out! Wherever this is the situation, the church is growing.

When Pastor Doug Swendseid, American Lutheran Church World Mission Secretary for East Asia, returned from visiting churches in the People's Republic of China, he reported on the growth of the church there, despite government opposition. Its growth reminds us of the New Testament church in the book of Acts.

"How do you explain this?" he asked an elderly, overworked, Chinese Christian pastor.

"There are two things," the pastor replied. "One is lay leadership. Because we have so few pastors, lay persons assume leadership in studying the Scriptures and in teaching it. The other reason is that people see how Christians care for one another" (*The Lutheran Standard*, Dec. 13, 1985).

Trained leaders are needed but not if they develop into an elite class of Christians which considers itself as superior to the lay Christian.

The danger lies in the development of a "clergy caste" which assumes absolute power over all of the so-called sacred areas of life. The church is in trouble whenever the clergy begins to think that they "own" the worship of the people of God, the teaching and preaching of the word of God, the ministry of Baptism and the Lord's Supper, and the "public" witness of the gospel.

Ministry and Christian vocation really occur in the everyday world of labor, marriage, and family life.

The church in the New Testament

To paint a picture of the church in the New Testament is virtually impossible with the few brushstrokes we're given by the writers of those books. Only Matthew records any usage of the word *church* by Jesus. Other than that we have a picture of Jesus as a rabbi, teaching his followers, both men and women, in small groups and in large crowds, demonstrating love and a ministry of service to all people.

He gave to those who followed him the benefit of a small, closely-knit community of people who slept with him, ate with him, dialoged with him, and who watched him perform signs and wonders. And then he died and rose again leaving them with the promise that they, that is, anyone who believed in him, would do the same works he did and "even greater things than these" (John 14:12).

According to the New Testament writings, they did as Jesus had promised them. But about church structures very little is said.

The apostle Paul compared the church to a living body, a family, a temple, a marriage, an army, a citizenry, and a household of faith in the letter to the Ephesians. A later letter to Timothy gives some criteria for the selection of lay bishops, deacons, elders, and the office of widow but that's about it.

The Spirit, Paul said, is the author of certain "gifts" for ministry and service in the church.

Little is said that speaks to today's denominational structures, the office of the papacy, and electronic churches! In these areas, we look to church tradition and history to help us.

And always, we go back to the earliest history, to our church "roots" to check our directions and, if necessary, to make course corrections.

Christian beginnings

Antioch in Syria is the place, we are told in the book of Acts, where the followers of Jesus Christ were first called "Christians" (11:19-26).

Obviously, there was something about those believers in Antioch that identified them unmistakably with Jesus Christ. So they were labeled "Christ-ians."

When we examine the reasons why the church at Antioch provoked this label from the residents of that city we learn some exciting things.

(1) Antioch Christians centered their lives in Jesus.

Labels and nicknames are often given as terms of

derision. Calling "Hey, you Christian!" to someone on the streets of Antioch was probably not a mark of love or respect.

Instead, it marked them as traitors, apostate Jews who were followers of an executed criminal. The label probably also implied that they were rather stupid persons for believing that a dead man could return to life, walk around the earth for 40 days and then disappear into the clouds with the promise that he would return again!

No one in Antioch could miss seeing that Jesus Christ was the center and the circumference of the life of these Christians. Everything they did was motivated by their conviction that he was the Promised One and their belief that his life and death and resurrection were the signs that God had not forgotten his people.

The followers of Jesus did not choose the name "Christian" for themselves but it appropriately indicated who they were and what, or who, they believed. As a result of the Antioch experience, the followers of Jesus Christ have been called by the name "Christian" ever since that time.

All other titles, names, or designations have only detracted from the Antioch nickname. Being called Nazarenes, Lutherans, Methodists, Anglicans, Catholics, Disciples, does not enhance the name given by the citizens of Antioch.

Unfortunately, even the word *Christian* has for many of us lost its original significance and become no more than an organizational designation of club membership, like Rotarian or Republican. We have done little to deserve the title in most cases.

As the church in the Western countries has become more acculturated, it's often enough just to be a citizen of North America or Europe to warrant being called a Christian.

Fortunately, that wasn't enough for the Christians in Antioch. So contagious was their witness that their community of faith grew to be a "great number" (Acts 11:21, 24).

(2) The church in Antioch was a lay people's church.

Lay persons founded the church in Antioch. They are identified as the people "who had been scattered by the persecution in connection with Stephen," in about A.D. 40.

The story of Stephen is told in Chapters 6 and 7 of Acts. This young man, the first Christian martyr, was stoned to death for a speech in which he identified Jesus as God's "Righteous One" who had been unjustly betrayed and murdered by his hearers.

Did you know that the Greek word *martyros* is translated into English as "witness"?

As a result of Stephen's witness and death, we are told that "a great persecution broke out against the church at Jerusalem and all except the apostles scattered throughout the region of Judea and Samaria." Note that the apostles were not among those who were "scattered" by the oppressors.

Why not the apostles? Were the authorities more fearful of the witness of lay people? Did they feel that they could control a few leaders but they were in trouble if the multitude of believers came alive and began to speak out against oppressive governments? Were they fearful of civil disobedience if everybody followed Stephen's example and spoke against sacred institutions like the Temple?

We pray in our churches for lay people to come alive but often when that happens, they become a threat to both church and political leadership.

A sleeping, uninvolved citizenry gives free reign to tyrants and demagogues. An apathetic laity, unwilling to expend any energy in support of its faith, not caring enough to give its witness for Christ, unenthusiastic about its commitments, will some day find itself as powerless as the "valley of dry bones"!

The true disciple does not confuse a pious life-style and a religious vocabulary with discipleship.

Lay people, living in the real world, are best able to discern if their church is no longer distinguishable from the culture in which it is planted and must then call it back to what it means to be salt and yeast in the world.

Lay people must do what leaders often cannot do.

The prophet Amos was a layman, a herdsman, and a cultivator of sycamore trees whose fruit was eaten mainly by poor people. He felt that his call was to be the champion of the poor who were being oppressed by a government which was supposed to be under the rule of God, a theocracy.

The priest Amaziah, in league with the king, tried to send Amos away with the words, "Don't prophesy anymore at Bethel, because this is the king's sanctuary and the temple of the kingdom" (Amos 7:13).

Amos told the priest that he was not a professional prophet but "the LORD took me from tending the flock" and kept on with his calling to warn "you who trample the needy and do away with the poor of the land."

Concerned lay people, ordinary Christians, in the 19th century were responsible for the evangelical revival and the organization of benevolence and missionary societies at a time when theologians were mired in debates over biblical criticism and the search for the historical Jesus. William Carey, a cobbler of shoes, opened India to the gospel. Mary Slessor, a Welsh factory girl, brought the message of Christ to unexplored areas of Africa. Dr. Fanny Butler founded the first hospital and medical training school in India.

Today, as in Antioch, the most effective way of spreading the good news may be to transplant groups of Christians to new neighborhoods and apartment complexes and let them become the seeds of new Christian fellowships.

(3) Antioch witnesses were willing to suffer for Christ.

Wherever lay people are willing to suffer for the sake of their witness, the church grows.

The early missionary enterprise in Madagascar was just limping along until a queen came into power determined to get rid of all Christians. Thousands of them were thrown over cliffs. Many could be heard singing as they were falling. Out of their joyous witness to the reality of the living Christ the church grew, doubling and redoubling with every Christian killed.

In the Ethiopian church, the number of Christians has increased dramatically since its oppression under the Marxist government.

Peter caught that sense of the name "Christian" in one of the only two other times the word is used in the New Testament when he said, "If you suffer as a Christian, do not be ashamed, but praise God that you bear that name" (1 Peter 4:16).

Is it appropriate to pose this question, If Christians are not witnessing in the countries of the West, is it because we are not willing to suffer as Christians? Have we so identified with our political systems that no one fears us enough to persecute us? Do the rewards of an often unjust economic system silence our witness?

Is that why the church is static and even decreasing in outreach and effectiveness?

Suffering does not have to be physical, however.

The most "alive" church we came across in England had experienced renewal through the spiritual awakening of both the rector and the people who began to use the gifts of all of the people in ministry both inside and outside of the church walls.

The "suffering" those church people experience arises from their alienation from other more traditional congregations who regard their signs of renewal as theologically suspect, if not objects of envy!

In our secular society any witness to the resurrection of Jesus Christ as a living reality will bring some suffering to the one who bears that witness.

The bodily resurrection of the dead is not a subject that's given much credence among intellectuals in our materialistic and scientific culture. The fear of suffering ridicule keeps many of us from witnessing to our faith in the Son of God.

Being laughed at and made to feel foolish in the eyes of educated and/or intelligent people involves real suffering for many. The apostle may have been feeling some of this when he wrote his first letter to the church in Corinth that "the message of the cross is foolishness to those who are perishing" (1:18) and later to the Romans to whom he asserted that he was "not ashamed of the gospel, because it is the power of God for the salvation of everyone who believes" (1:16).

(4) Antioch Christians created an inclusive church.

Those early Jewish Christians spoke primarily to other Jews about the Jewish Messiah, Jesus the Christ. Sociologists tell us that people tend to associate with people like themselves.

The gospel dynamic, however, cuts across sociological norms.

Some of the converts who came to Antioch from the islands of Cyprus and Cyrene, immediately spoke to Gentiles (non-Jews) also.

When the news came to "headquarters" at Jerusalem that Antioch Christians were enlisting a "great number" of Gentiles, the Jewish Christian leadership in that city sent a man named Barnabas to investigate.

Thank God that Barnabas was a man "full of the Holy Spirit and faith." As such he saw this inclusiveness as "evidence of the grace of God" and affirmed the wisdom and actions of the church.

Unless the church actively reaches out to people of all races it will eventually become an ineffective witness.

Any *apartheid* practices in the congregations in the United States are suspect, since we live in a land which welcomes people of all nations into its population.

(5) The Antioch church emphasized mission outreach.

After the fall of Jerusalem to the Romans and the destruction of the Temple there in the year A.D. 70, Antioch became the acknowledged center for missionary outreach. Long before that time the apostle Paul had started his missionary journeys from that city (Acts 13:1-3).

Matthew's gospel is thought to have originated out of the Antioch church where he may later have made his home. If his gospel were written from Antioch, that affirms the missionary character of the Antioch church.

The missionary word at the close of Matthew's gospel is inclusive and universal, with its injunction to "Go and make disciples of all nations" (28:19-20).

The New Testament church, like the church in Africa today, drew its vitality and its ability to draw people into its fellowship from Spirit-led lay people who were at the forefront of its witness.

They founded a church community, not with fixed structures and rigid doctrinal positions, but with the powerful assurance that Jesus Christ was alive and that his presence had sustained them through persecution and suffering.

4

THE NAME OF JESUS

Τhis is really Chantal's chapter.

When I met her, she was three years old and lived in Africa.

When we landed in Bangui in the Central African Republic we faced a seven hour journey up to Gallo, the first missionary station we were scheduled to visit. We would be riding, we learned, with Carl and Paula Stecker and their two children, Chantal, 3, and Alyssa, 9 months, all of whom met us at the airport.

Carl and Paula are both nurses, graduates of a church-related college in the United States. They work, not in connection with a mission hospital, but out in the "bush," bringing medical care to the people who have no ready access to a hospital.

"We'll stay in a hotel in Bangui tonight," they informed us, "and leave as soon as we can after breakfast in order to get to Gallo before dark. But first of all we have to pick up groceries and other supplies to take back to the station."

One of the pieces they had to pick up was a motor. When Carl went to the equipment warehouse to get it, the electricity in that part of the city was turned off for two hours due to the shortage of hydroelectric power during the dry season.

So we got off to a late start.

Since roads in that part of the country were made of red dirt, packed hard but rutted and potholed, one could expect some delays.

Our friends did not tell us that one of the most common accidents on those roads was the shattering of windshields by rocks thrown from the wheels of passing vehicles. And that's exactly what happened to us when we were about three hours away from our destination.

One of the many overloaded, top-heavy trucks trying to pass us on the narrow road threw a rock as it went by and the windshield of our pickup shattered in thousands of pieces.

When we stopped along the road to pick the rest of the glass out of the car and the rubber gasket around the windshield, Carl commented that the rainy season had apparently already started in that area.

"That's good," said we, in our ignorance. "Then we won't get so much dust in the car." By this time we and all of the contents in the car were covered with fine red dust.

Our hosts wisely did not tell us that the rains usually brought out more bugs and that they especially released termites in flying swarms by the millions.

As darkness fell with tropical swiftness, our inno-cent delight over the dustless road dispelled quickly as the headlights beamed the winged termites right into the large opening where the windshield used to be! The termites smashed into our mouths, our noses, crawled in our hair, smeared our glasses, and found their way inside our blouses and shirts.

Since there are no roadside inns, motels, hotels, or bed and breakfast places out in the African countryside, we drove on.

Chantal was sitting in my lap. I said, "Chantal, do you think we could praise God for the termites?"

I really wasn't sure what good that would do, but I remembered reading about Corrie ten Boom and her sister in the book *The Hiding Place* who praised God for the fleas that infested their persons, clothing, and beds in the Nazi concentration camp in which they were imprisoned.

Chantal apparently thought this a perfectly reasonable suggestion and said, "I know a song about praising Jesus!"

The rest of us had our mouths covered to keep the termites from flying into them but Chantal opened her mouth and in a clear childish soprano started to sing her song of praise to Jesus.

And the termites stopped coming.

I mean, they really stopped.

Her father said, "It probably hasn't rained here."

He was probably right.

Then again, maybe the termites had stopped coming because Chantal believed that a song of praise to Jesus could keep them out of our car.

Faith like a child

How do we recapture the naturalness of Chantal-like faith?

How can we let Jesus come so close that he becomes our second nature?

How do we let ourselves be so overwhelmed by the glory of Jesus that the same childlike faith will sing in us with Chantal's absolute conviction that Jesus can change things?

The apostles Peter and John attributed their post-resurrection power to their faith in the "name" of Jesus. When a lame beggar asked them for some money, they told him they didn't have any money but they had something else to give him. "In the name of Jesus Christ of Nazareth, walk," they said, and he did (Acts 3:6).

When people were amazed and stared at them (as if making a lame man walk was something unusual!) Peter told them that the name of Jesus itself had power to heal and give perfect health.

All one had to do was to have faith in that name, he said.

That's childlike faith, isn't it?

But if one knows the person represented by the name, then the faith is justified.

Peter had been with Jesus for three years. During that time he had seen him release multitudes of people from their crippling and crying needs.

He saw Jesus bring hope into the hopelessness of a thousand despairs.

Because Peter had seen, he believed. His faith in the name of Jesus was based on actual eyewitness knowledge of the person behind the name.

A disciple named Thomas said he would not believe Jesus was raised from the dead unless he actually touched the wounds in Jesus' hands and side. Indeed, he *could not* believe, without physical proof that the one who claimed to have been raised from the dead was really the same man who had been nailed to the cross. It was then that Jesus gave him his "proof" but told him, "Blessed are those who have not seen and yet have believed" (John 20:24-29).

Childlike faith is not based on experience.

Faith in the name of Jesus is faith in all that the name promises. "Blessed are those who have not seen and yet have believed."

There's something about that name

Even our names mean quite a bit to us.

We sign a name to a document and unbelievable things happen just as a result of that simple act. Houses transfer ownership, debts are contracted and paid off, marriages are made and broken, great fortunes are gained and lost. All because a name is signed.

When I want my husband or child to come, I call their names and they answer. I invoke their presence by calling their names.

The invocation at the beginning of worship calls out the names of the deity to assure the worshipers of God's presence among them.

The power to change lives and circumstances is in the name of Jesus.

The name of Jesus saves. "If you confess with your mouth, 'Jesus is Lord,' and believe in your heart that God raised him from the dead, you will be saved" (Rom. 10:9).

The name of Jesus is above every name and at the name of Jesus "every knee should bow, in heaven and on earth" (Phil. 2:9-10).

Forgiveness is in the name of Jesus. Peter told the people whose hearts were touched by his Pentecost message to "be baptized, every one of you, in the name of

Jesus Christ" and they would find forgiveness of their sins (Acts 2:38).

The name of Jesus confronts the demons that inhabit our world. Confronted by Jesus, the demons knew his name and were frightened. "What do you want with us, Jesus of Nazareth?" they cried out. "Have you come to destroy us? I know who you are—the Holy One of God" (Mark 1:24).

The name of Jesus contains and transfers his mysterious person and power to the one who speaks it and permits the power in his name to give energy to those who hear it spoken.

Jesus, Jesus, Jesus, sweetest name I know. . . .

Jesus, Jesus, Jesus, there's something about that name. . . .

Jesus, name above all names. . . .

The name has been sung and spoken in a thousand different tongues, in hundreds of arrangements and melodies, in praise, in distress, in pain, in supplication, in death, in worship, in triumph.

For Christians, nothing seems to surpass the joy of being able to sing or say, "Jesus."

In the biblical witness the name unveils all of the qualities of God's person. The name is not magic but it produces what it promises.

We think of the hundreds of people we've known whose lives have been transformed by that name. Nothing has been more satisfying in our experience than to have known the host of people who have been enabled to live joyously because of that name.

The name of Jesus makes it possible for us to sing in the middle of the most fearsome circumstances. For Chantal, just a little girl, the night was dark and the road lonely. Few cars travel on African roads at night. The insects of the night were so persistent and disturbing. She sensed the worries of her father who, at one point, told us that he wasn't sure he could keep going any longer.

Chantal believed that Jesus, whose name she praised, could change all of this.

The name, spoken by one who has faith in the name, releases its own creative power.

The powers of evil in our world would like to suppress the name of Jesus for that reason.

"By what power or what name did you do this?" the authorities in Jerusalem challenged Peter and John (Acts 4:7).

When they were told that the lame man was made whole and given perfect health in the name of Jesus, that it was faith in his name that had raised him up, the authorities did what you would expect them to do.

They ordered the disciples "not to speak or teach at all in the name of Jesus" (Acts 4:18).

Suppress the name! Don't permit people to talk about Jesus. That's the way to keep resurrection power from working its good news in the lives of people and institutions.

Witnessing and evangelization begin with people who believe that there is power in the name of Jesus to change life for themselves and for others. They accept the promised power that the Holy Spirit was sent to give them (Acts 1:8). They know that they are not going to witness in their own power.

Our witness starts when we permit ourselves to be so drawn to Jesus that we cannot help but talk about him whenever we can.

"For to me, to live is Christ," we say with Paul (Phil. 1:21), and we want others to have this ecstatic assurance.

If we want a church that lives in our world with resurrection power, we who are the people called "Christians" will have to start speaking the name of Jesus unashamedly and with Chantal-like faith in its power to change the people and the circumstances with which we are living.

As a friend of Jesus, remember his name.

Talk about him often.

——— 5

THE PROBLEM OF AMNESIA

We need to witness as much for our own sake as for the sake of others.

We have often been exhorted to witness to others so that *they* can have a chance to hear the good news and be "saved."

If that's the only reason why I should witness, then, I might reason, if I know that people have plenty of other opportunities to hear the gospel, why should I bother to talk to them about Jesus?

I need to talk about him for my sake, to help me remember all that he has done for me, to remind me of his grace in my own life.

Jesus changed my life. Without him, God only knows where I would be today.

I don't want to forget that.

Talking to others about him will keep my own memory of him alive.

What we don't use we lose

Medical people tell us this about the functions of our bodies. Atrophy, a wasting away process, occurs in parts that are unused. Memories grow dim and are soon forgotten when they are never recalled to our consciousness.

Every year, at 3:30 P.M. on August 10, my husband and I find a place to sit and talk about an event that radically changed our lives at that time some years ago. On that date, his neck was broken in a body surfing accident. He was totally paralyzed and was told that he would never walk again.

We never want to forget how that verdict was translated into the restoration of his body and the ability to walk again. So on every anniversary of his ocean accident, we talk about it, recalling every detail of that time and place, every feeling, every word.

He tells the story from his point of view and I tell it from my perspective. We particularly remind each other of the action of God's Spirit in our lives at that time. We praise God and celebrate the bonus years after our death and re-birth in the salt waters of the Pacific Ocean.

Married couples do the same thing when they celebrate the anniversaries of their wedding day. Pictures are taken out, friends and members of the wedding party are invited to share the festivities in remembrance of the occasion.

As friends talk about that time, sharing stories and anecdotes, husband and wife experience again the love and joy of that remembered moment. Their marriage vows are renewed and they can fall in love all over again.

When couples come to us for help with a troubled marriage, one of the healing techniques is to recall with them the feelings they had for each other in the early days of their courtship. What was it in the other one that made them feel excited about being together?

As pictures of those moments take shape in their memories, positive feelings about their relationship may be aroused that counteract some of the negative feelings that have accumulated more recently.

The importance of remembering

When people can't remember who or where they are, they suffer from a frightening condition called amnesia. When people become insane they lose touch with the realities of time and space.

We all have friends who become quite anxious when they cannot remember the name of a person or a place that they know well. They fear that senility or some dreadful disease may be starting.

Other people pride themselves on their ability to remember birthdays, anniversaries, and addresses.

Some spend a lot of money attending seminars that guarantee to increase one's ability to remember names and appointments. A variety of strategies and gimmicks are employed to stimulate the functions of memory.

How flattered we are when an important person remembers us and can call us by name even though many years have elapsed since our last encounter!

We query, "Remember me?" and put people in a somewhat embarrassing position if they don't remember us.

A certain public speaker was even endowed with great saintliness because it was rumored that he never forgot the name of a person he had met at a meeting even though as a popular speaker he had met thousands every year!

In a sense, we are what we remember.

The memory of God

God *remembers.*

God remembers our names. "Fear not, for I have redeemed you; I have summoned you by name; you are mine" (Isa. 43:1).

God remembers promises. "I will remember my covenant between me and you and all living creatures of every kind," God promised Noah. "Never again will the waters become a flood to destroy all life" (Gen. 9:15).

God remembers people caught in distressful situations.

After Noah had spent hundreds of days floating in a smelly boat full of animals "God remembered Noah and all the wild animals and all the livestock that were with him in the ark" (Gen. 8:1). When God remembered, God did something about the mess Noah was in.

"[God] sent a wind over the earth, and the waters receded."

When the people of Israel were groaning under their slavery in Egypt and crying out for help, their cry came up to God. "God heard their groaning and he remembered his covenant with Abraham, with Isaac and with Jacob" (Exod. 2:23-24). With the memory, God proceeded with a plan to release the remembered ones from bondage.

God remembers those who suffer.

When the beloved Rachel was suffering pain because her sister had six sons and one daughter and she had none in a society that valued women for their ability to bear children, "then God remembered Rachel . . . and opened her womb" (Gen. 30:22).

God remembers those who pray.

When the cities of Sodom and Gomorrah were to be destroyed, Abraham prayed that his nephew Lot would not die along with the other dwellers in those cities. God promised that Lot would be saved if there were only 10 people faithful to God among the people.

"So when God destroyed the cities of the plain, he remembered Abraham, and brought Lot out of the catastrophe that overthrew the cities" (Gen. 19:29).

Remembering is essential to faith

God knows that remembering is essential to our faith. When we forget, we run the risk of losing our entire heritage. Through the prophets, God tried to revive in the memories of the people of Israel Yahweh's faithfulness and love.

When they chose instead to forget God, they were given the word that "like a wind from the east, I will scatter them" (Jer. 18:17).

When they forgot what God had done for them, the Israelites were always in trouble.

The primary memory they were always to keep was their liberation from the bondage of slavery in Egypt.

To help them remember, God gave them a special meal called the Passover meal. They were to celebrate every anniversary of their escape from slavery by eating the Passover. No matter where they were in the world, they would eat the Passover as a witness to their memory of God's goodness in delivering them from slavery and death in Egypt.

Christians are people whose memories center around the cross of Calvary, the place of their deliverance from the slavery to sin and death.

To help us remember, Jesus served his disciples a special meal of bread and wine during their celebration of the Passover meal and he told them that this was the bread and the wine of the "new covenant," signs of his body and blood given for the forgiveness of their sins.

"Do this!" he commanded.

The act of eating and drinking was to be "in remembrance" of him and their witness to his death. "For whenever you eat this bread and drink this cup, you proclaim the Lord's death until he comes" (1 Cor. 11:26).

In the act of eating and drinking, their memory of him would be refreshed and sharpened and the memory of his life and death renewed. Do this, and every time you do it, no matter how often, it will be in remembrance of Jesus and a witness to his crucifixion.

If you stop doing it or don't do it often enough, hardening of your spiritual arteries will set in and eventually your memory and your faith will fade.

Remembering is the result of sensory stimulation. An action in the present recalls all of the former event in its totality. All of the implications of the occasion or life of a person remembered are relived with all of the emotions associated with them.

The whole of Jesus' ministry, his death and resurrection, are focused in the *act* of eating the Lord's Supper. Thus we memorialize the event.

Witnessing keeps our memory of Jesus alive

In the act of witnessing to others we keep alive our memory of God's actions on our behalf. The event of our own personal liberation from whatever slavery chained us revives in our memory every time we tell someone about it.

Compared to some people's stories, our own may seem quite ordinary and uninteresting, but our story is our witness and is uniquely our own.

I've often thought my own witness would be much more dramatic and make for more exciting reading or hearing if it included past encounters with crime or drug addiction, alcoholism, or prostitution! People who have had those kinds of experiences *know* what they've been delivered from, it seems.

I recently read the fearful story of a man who was delivered from demonism and years of attacks by dark forces of evil. Now he warns people of the dangers in magic, fortune-telling, and the practice of witchcraft.

I cannot include any of the above experiences in my history.

Therefore, my witness does not include anything as exciting as deliverance from those slaveries.

Mine is an unexciting, ordinary story.

Even my childhood was ordinary. My parents lived together for 56 years until my father died. No child abuse or feelings of being unwanted lie buried in my psyche. My parents gave evidence of love and affection to each other and to each one of their eight children and seemed to value us as gifted human beings capable of the highest achievement.

Every attempt was made to enrich our lives even though we struggled financially on a truck driver's salary. We took tennis lessons at the park, piano lessons in school, violin lessons in the band and orchestra, entered spelling contests and math tournaments, and made daily trips to the public libraries in Chicago.

We had the necessities of life, we had love, we had health and opportunity.

So why, then, was I often depressed and anxious? Why did I feel alone and as though life had little meaning for me?

Why, underneath my laughter, was there a voice that often whispered, "There's not much point in living, is there?"

Of course, there was the Great Depression and the city was generally bleak in outlook, but I had been baptized, I sang in a choir, was active in a church youth group, and I had even gotten a job in a bank in downtown Chicago. Wasn't that supposed to do it?

Even so, for one terrifying year of my life, I fought against the ever-present urge to kill myself.

Then I was given a job at a Christian college and the opportunity to go to school there.

The witness that made the difference for me

It was the witness of one student in particular that made the difference in my life.

Again, I have nothing dramatic to report.

He was a young man from a small midwestern town and had to work as hard as I did to pay his college bills.

Life did not seem to offer him any more than it offered me. But there was a freedom about him that I wished I had. He seemed to have none of the fears and inhibitions that plagued me. Instead he radiated a positive joy and contagious enthusiasm that, while I sometimes resented it, drew me to him.

I think I said something sarcastic the first time he told me that Jesus could make a difference in my life. But I couldn't stop thinking about him and what he said and I kept coming back with more questions and more objections.

I expected him to tell me some fantastic conversion story when I asked him how he had come to this "faith" and I was fully prepared to cross it all off as evidence of some kooky fanaticism.

Instead, he simply said, "I don't remember ever *not* believing in Jesus. I think I've believed in him ever since I was baptized."

"I've been baptized and I believe in Jesus," I told him. "How come I don't feel the same way you do?"

THE POWER OF ORDINARY CHRISTIANS ████████████

"I don't know," he answered. "Maybe you don't want to accept all that being a follower of Jesus Christ demands."

What did that mean?

Amazing grace

His words continued to bother me. I didn't even want to talk to him after that. I avoided him and dismissed him from my thoughts by putting him in a box labeled "Religious Fanatic."

Since we worked in the same college office, I found myself working furiously whenever he was around so that I wouldn't be forced to engage in conversation with him.

Finally, the tension which was building in me had to be released. I felt torn between a fear of death and a fear of living.

One night, walking alone across the darkened summer campus, I simply said out loud (to whom, I don't know), "I give up. I don't know what's the matter with me, but I don't want to go on living like this any longer."

At that moment, it seemed to me that the campus around me was filled with light. I felt surrounded by the presence of God and I knew that Jesus was real and living. *How* I knew, I can't say, but the fact that I knew was validated by the change that came into my emotions, my thinking, my outlook on life in general.

Angels accompanied me across the campus, I felt, and I stayed awake most of the rest of that night thinking about what had happened, praying, singing, and wondering. I experienced a desire to read the Bible in a hungry sort of way, something I had never experienced before.

The change in my life was evident to my friends. Some of them didn't like what I had become. They preferred me as I had been. They didn't like the "me" who wanted to talk about what had happened and the difference that happening had made in me.

I found myself drawn to a great many of the people I had felt repelled by before, including the young man who had witnessed to me, and I withdrew from others who had attracted me before.

I told my friend what had happened to me that night on the campus but, for some perverse reason, I refused to admit even to myself that he had anything to do with that experience.

I wanted to claim it as my own.

And, of course, it was, and is, my own experience. Others can react in whatever way they want to react, just as I reacted to my friend's witness, but for me that's how Jesus came alive for me and how change came into my life.

Telling about my experience makes Jesus real in the present

I've told my story many times to a variety of people in a number of places and under a wide range of circumstances. I don't tell it to everybody and I confess to feeling a bit foolish writing it in this book.

But I need to tell it often enough to keep my own memory of that grace-filled night in my own history alive for me. When I haven't had an occasion to tell it to someone for a long time, I find myself subject to doubts about the reality of Christ's death *for me.*

I lose the sense of joy that always bubbles in me when the memory of my encounter with Jesus is kept fresh.

Like the apostle John, I must proclaim that which I've "heard" and "seen" so that "you also may have fellowship with us" and I "write this to make our joy complete."

Practice helps

If you are not used to talking about what Jesus means to you, you probably will find this a difficult assignment: Start today by telling your story to someone!

Try to avoid talking about your church and its activities. Concentrate on Jesus and what he has done for all people and for you. Your story is as valid a witness as anyone else's. It may be as simple as my friend's saying that he knew Jesus since his Baptism.

You can't control anyone else's reaction to your story.

But telling it will refresh your memory of God's grace in your life.

It may remind you that you're out of practice in your witness and that you had better get reacquainted with Jesus Christ and rediscover your vocation in him.

If you don't have anything to say about Jesus, why not?

Are you overlooking something quite obvious in yourself that others see but you don't? Perhaps a friend can point out a "witness" you're already making but that you are not aware of yourself.

For example, it was the joyousness of my friend that was his chief witness to me. His words simply pointed to the Source of his joy.

We've mentioned "joy" a number of times now in connection with stories of faith. Joy seems to be the distinguishing characteristic of the person whose life is lived "in Christ."

Theologian Teilhard de Chardin said that "joy is the surest sign of the Presence of God."

Seventy times in the New Testament Christians are called to "Rejoice!"

"I want what she's got" a woman said when asked why she wanted to join the church. She was referring to Jean who had not had an easy life, but who definitely had joy! The woman attributed Jean's joy to her affiliation with a Christian church.

Joy results from one's experience of God's overwhelming love. It cannot be contained and must overflow into every meeting with others. When one's witness is validated by joy it's an irresistible force drawing others to Jesus Christ.

You can tell people why you're joyous, can't you? We're not talking just about smiling and making jokes or anything superficial but about the sustaining joy that transforms and transcends pain and sorrow and all other adversities.

That's your witness.

Did you think it was more complicated than that? Did you think you had to have courses in theology or know every verse in the Bible by heart?

Actually, you don't even have to be able to read or write to be able to witness. It's simply this, "whatever you do, whether in word or deed, do it all in the name of the Lord Jesus" (Col. 3:17).

Are you helping someone who needs help? If they ask why you bother, tell them it's because you love them like Jesus loves you.

If they ask why you go to church can you tell them that Jesus said "where two or three come together" in his name, that's where he is, too? (Matt. 18:20).

Our churches will not come alive until members can name the name of Jesus and so keep alive their own joy in what Jesus means to them.

That's contagious! That's powerful! That's transforming!

Create opportunities to witness

What kind of witnessing opportunities can you arrange?

A woman who had just moved to New Jersey had been active in the work of Lutheran World Relief. In a new neighborhood without old friends to visit, she determined to create her own fellowship and also to use it as an opportunity to witness to what was happening around the world in the name of Jesus.

She began by sending formal invitations to her neighbors to a morning get-together for the purpose of introducing herself to them and in turn getting acquainted with them.

When they came they noticed the quilting blocks she "just happened" to have lying on her work table. Of course this was her opportunity to explain her involvement in world relief efforts. Her neighbors, who obviously were women who were not employed outside the home, asked if they could help.

Soon Jan had 18 women coming regularly to help sew quilts! They also learned a great deal about the motivating power behind Christians who are compelled by the love of Christ to help others.

Be prepared when opportunities come

For those who are employed outside the home, or who volunteer in the many organizations at work in our society, the opportunities to witness are endless.

What you do and who you are will probably influence your witness in those situations. Joy, love, peace, and openness to people are the qualities that attract others. They open doors to us through which others can walk.

Then, as Paul told Philemon, "I pray that you may be active in sharing your faith, so that you will have a full understanding of every good thing we have in Christ" (Philemon 6).

For you, there will be a renewal of joy as you refresh the memory of your story.

Without that frequent sharing, you may lose your witness and with it the joy that it brought into your life. The reality of Jesus will grow dim, melting into the 2000-year-old history recorded in the Scriptures.

Those who need your witness will be impoverished and you, in turn, may suffer spiritual amnesia.

"Do this," says the Lord, "in remembrance of me."

It's in the act of taking the Lord's Supper that the events of Christ's acts in history are brought into the present.

It's in the act of witnessing that the memory of what Jesus has done in my life is brought into the present for me.

6

COME TO CHURCH WITH ME

We need to belong, to be bonded to others.

Native Americans have reminded us of our interconnectedness with all of creation. The trees, the animals, the rivers, the mountains—they affirm—are all part of our being, they are our brothers and sisters.

Because we had come to feel a strong bond with the African people we had met on our journey there, we grieved when we left those countries because of what is happening to the close ties of tribe and family as urbanization and Western "progress" come to disrupt traditional structures of society.

So far, those ancient ties have remained intact in the rural areas. As we drove through the dark countryside at night, the light of a thousand cooking fires outside the doors of huts signaled the end of the day's labors and the gathering of the family for the evening meal.

Those bright spots in the gloom of night were symbols of the unbroken bonds of family and community.

Cars, electricity, and jobs in the cities will be pulling apart the communities of Africa just as the products of progress have severed traditional family ties in the United States and forced us to make new connections.

Making new connections

Author Kurt Vonnegut has a character in his book *Slaughterhouse Five* who writes a book in which the president of the United States travels to Nigeria, where he is impressed by the extended family way of caring for each other.

When the president comes home, he announces a new plan for making everyone in the United States a member of an extended family! The computers of the Social Security Administration are going to assign everybody thousands of relatives by giving them the same middle name.

In his spoof of government and family, Vonnegut still recognized the need for human connections. We need each other for all kinds of reasons, emotional, social, physical, spiritual.

For the Christian the new connection is Jesus. His name ties us all together in a new connectedness called the "church."

This church is the "called-out" family, *ecclesia* in New Testament Greek, whose members all have the same new "middle" name!

Anyone can become a member of this new family, this new community. It has no geographic boundaries, owes allegiance to no one political structure, lives under dictatorships, under oppressive regimes, in democracies and monarchies. All skin colors are represented among its members and it includes poor and rich alike.

Wherever you travel on the face of this planet you will find members of your new family. We all have the same middle name at the center of our being.

Wanted: invitations

Most of us come into the church by invitation. Somehow we have to be made to know that we're welcome.

An invitation is often the first step on the way to new life and new connections.

Someone says, "Will you come to church with me?"

With that invitation someone offers another person a whole new set of possibilities for community and belonging, for love and caring.

John Dewey, once my colleague in ministry to congregations, tells the story of two neighbors who met every Sunday morning at the same time as they were getting their cars out of their garages. The one threw his bag of golf clubs into the trunk, the other drove off to church. Every Sunday the golfer would invite his neighbor to go golfing with him. His neighbor always said, "No, I'm on my way to church."

Finally, the golfer said to the churchgoer, "I've invited you many times to go to the golf course with me. How come you never ask me to go to church with you?"

Indeed, why didn't the churchgoer invite his neighbor to church with him?

R.S.V.P.

Our responsibility and privilege is *to ask*. That's all. The response is up to the one invited.

If that person says no, then what?

Well, you can invite again. And again, if necessary.

If the person says yes, that may be the beginning of a whole new relationship for both of you as neighbors and friends and as members of the fellowship of people with the same middle name.

I've told you my story, my witness to what Jesus means to me in the previous chapter, but that's only half of my story.

The first part of the story begins many years before that, about one month after I was born. That's when my parents took me to a church to be baptized. The place was a neighborhood Presbyterian chapel in what is now the inner city of Chicago. I don't even know if it's still in existence. At that time my mother was attending that church and my father was a Roman Catholic.

Like many other couples in which each partner was brought up in a different Christian denomination, they weren't sure how that division of loyalties should be handled in the lives of their children.

Both of them, however, were convinced that their primary loyalty was to Jesus Christ and they were determined not to let church structures divide them and alienate their children.

They fostered in us a love of God, the Word, and the church that went beyond their particular church membership traditions.

They decided, after some struggles, that their children would not join either church but would always attend a Protestant congregation closest to the place they were living at the time. Since we moved frequently that made for a good bit of variety in our church experience!

All of this may sound quite strange to some of you who were brought up in one particular denominational tradition but it gave me a sense of the oneness and yet diversity which marks the Christian community around the world.

We observed that some churches were more serious, some more pious, some more fun. We received the Lord's Supper sitting in pews, standing up front, kneeling at the altar. All pastors seemed more alike than different with minor variations in their garments.

That's the way church went for us until I was 10 years old. Then a two-and-a-half-year-old brother died and at the same time my mother was hospitalized and almost died of the same kidney infection which claimed his life.

For some years after that we did not go to church. My father faithfully attended his weekly mass. My mother, grieving, seemed not to have the strength to get all of us ready for Sunday school and church.

In the meantime, the death of my little brother filled me with many unanswered, and largely unasked, questions.

I was angry with God (*If there was one,* I thought) for taking my brother to be with him in heaven, as my adult relatives told me. What right did God have to snatch him away from us?

And I felt guilty. I could not forgive myself for those times when the little boy had wanted to play with me and I had other things to do. I remembered the times I had hidden from him so that he couldn't find me, especially when I had a book I wanted to read.

I entered my teen years with recurring feelings of sadness and despair. God seemed far away, if around at all, and life and death seemed equally pointless in a meaningless existence.

The inviter

In my older brother's first year in high school a friend of his invited him to a neighborhood church's youth group. By an interesting coincidence it was a former pastor of this congregation who had been called to conduct the funeral service for my little brother.

Every week after that invitation we went to the youth group meetings at the local Lutheran church, primarily because they had a Ping-Pong table in the church basement.

The pastor was a very good Ping-Pong player.

He challenged us to beat him at the game. Then, he said, we would be eligible to join the youth organization.

Since he was a very good player, that meant we had to go to the church building to practice at other times during the week. While we were there, we were sometimes invited to help do things like mow the lawn, clip bushes, shovel snow, or go to the local ice cream parlor for a treat.

One by one our younger brothers and sisters started coming to Sunday school and to the youth meetings. One by one we beat the pastor at Ping-Pong after months of coming to practice.

During all of this time no one in the church ever criticized us "neighborhood kids" for not joining the church or told us that we couldn't come because our parents neither belonged nor contributed to the church budget.

Instead, we were invited to participate in all of the activities as though we were actually members.

One by one, under a seemingly unconscious, but very astute, evangelistic effort on the part of the entire congregation, we were made part of that loving fellowship.

We went through confirmation classes but were not allowed to be confirmed until we "were old enough to make our own decision."

And still we were loved and welcomed. The pastor came to our home and seemed genuinely to enjoy his visits with my Catholic father and my mother who was too busy at that time with her eight children to go to church. She also felt, at that time, that she could not afford the clothes needed to be presentable in church.

We were "family," part of the shared life of that fellowship.

When the pastor's son went to Luther College in Iowa, the pastor contacted the school and got a job for my brother so that he could go, too.

That's when I was working in the bank in downtown Chicago and had given up hope of ever going to college. The pastor had not forgotten me, however, and when he heard that there was an opening for a secretary to the college president, he recommended me.

And it all began with an invitation.

My brother was invited by a friend to go to his church.

My brother invited me.

I brought my sister.

By the time our youngest siblings were ready for the youth group, the whole family, mother and father included, had taken instruction and were members of the church!

We belonged. We became members of the global family with the same middle name.

What is your church's "public face"?

While studies indicate that most people come to the church as the result of loving and persistent invitations from church people who have become their neighbors and friends, they also tell us that people stay in a church because of the attitudes they meet when they get there.

Dr. Win Arn of the Institute for American Church Growth in Pasadena, California, surveyed 8600 persons in 39 Protestant denominations and concluded that most of the churches that attract people have "learned how to love." Congregations seeking to attract members "should concentrate less on pastoral leadership, attractiveness of facilities, location, liberal versus conservative theology, and evangelistic fervor, and more on how well they love" (*The Lutheran Standard,* Nov. 21, 1986).

From the pastors, people expect good preaching and teaching and loving, caring acceptance. From the people they expect authentic hospitality and a warm, nonjudgmental welcome.

They expect the congregation to have its priorities in the right order: people before property, persons before position and economic resources.

In the loving church, children are valued and their needs met. No one becomes annoyed when children make sounds during the worship service, but, at the same time, facilities are provided for their care elsewhere, should the parents want that.

Concern for the person's whole life must be the primary goal of the church's "loving" and not the addition of numbers to the membership list.

Gathering and koinonia

The gathering of the people seems to be the basic element in the life of the church. We are called out in order to come together as the people of God. Jesus, describing the church, focused on the gathering, when he told his disciples that "where two or three come together in my name, there am I with them" (Matt.18:20).

We are called out to participate in a common sharing of the Word, and the Lord's Supper, and Baptism, and to participate in the corporate life of prayer that lifts up the whole of humanity to the grace of God.

Although the church has a strong and fixed center in Jesus Christ, its perimeter is elastic and flexible. Baptism is an "inclusive" act that brings people into the fellowship, the *koinonia* of the church.

The *ecclesia* of the New Testament, "the assembly of called-out ones," never erects a barrier to exclude people. Just the opposite is true. Rather, it invites people by affirming that "all of you who were baptized into Christ have clothed yourselves with Christ. There is neither Jew nor Greek, slave nor free, male nor female for you are all one in Christ Jesus" (Gal. 3:27-28).

The call is never to separateness but always to oneness.

Denominations stand in contrast to the church of the New Testament.

Because the trend toward divisiveness was already appearing by the time Paul wrote his first letter to the Corinthian church in about A.D. 55, he wrote that "some from Chloe's household have informed me that there are quarrels among you. What I mean is this: One of you says, 'I follow Paul'; another, 'I follow Apollos'; another, 'I follow Cephas'; still another, 'I follow Christ.' Is Christ divided? Was Paul crucified for you? Were you baptized into the name of Paul?" (1 Cor. 1:11-13).

Nevertheless, our invitations to people must, as a reality, be to a particular congregation in a particular locality, in order for them to participate in the life of the people of God. Our ultimate goal, however, must constantly be to open the doors of our fellowship, our *koinonia* to all people, asking for their presence and participation in the life of Christ as it is expressed through that local gathering.

The task then becomes one of making our local con-gregation into the finest expression of the *ecclesia* that we can in order that Christ may be seen as its heart and center.

When ordinary Christians come alive with this pas-sion, their church will become a living center of love, drawing people into itself and connecting them to Jesus Christ and the gathered community in a new and re-newing extended family.

Isn't this the kind of church to which you would be eager to invite everyone?

7

WELCOME TO THE FELLOWSHIP!

The moment has come.

You've invited a friend to church many times and at last the answer is yes.

Even though you've had many opportunities to discuss your faith with your friend and know that your witness had made a difference in your friend's life, you also know that eventually this friend, like you, must become part of a Christian fellowship.

Now you're concerned because you know how important one's first impression of a church worship service can be. What will your friend think about the experience?

You've arranged to pick your guest up so that you can walk into church together. You know how hard it is for people to walk into a strange situation by themselves. In fact, you've been told that only three percent of the people who join a church were "walk-ins" or people who came the first time without a previous contact, a personal invitation, or someone to bring them.

Some anxiety about the reception your church peers will give your friend gnaws away at your composure.

Put yourself in the stranger's place

Your memory takes you back to the time you were on a business trip and on Sunday morning you decided to attend a church close to the hotel. The memory of that morning raises your anxiety level even more.

When you went to that church, you were met at the door by an usher who asked you if you were a "couple." When you said no, you were alone, he asked you to return the bulletin he had handed you because, as he said, "We only have enough copies for every two people today."

You recall the combined feelings of anger and amusement that struggled within you. You almost turned away to go back to the hotel but decided that after such an inauspicious beginning you had to see what the rest of the service would be like!

Things did not get better.

Without a bulletin you had no idea where the clergyman was leading the congregation. However, when you looked around, not many of the people in the pews (which were about 60% empty) looked like they knew or cared what was going on.

The pastor did not announce the hymn numbers and there was no hymnboard visible so you could not sing most of the hymns. One hymn was familiar and you found it in the index of the hymnal and sang along. Since this was the only opportunity you had had thus far to participate in the service you got rather carried away and sang more heartily than you normally did. When a few heads turned toward you as if wondering what had aroused such enthusiasm for one of the hymns, you recall smiling rather apologetically at one of the questioning faces and you sang the rest of the hymn in a more acceptably subdued manner.

You stood when others stood, and you sat when they sat.

After the service was over people gathered around a table set with coffee and donuts. One man with a *Deacon* badge on his lapel said "Good morning" with a nice smile and then returned to his conversation with two other people.

No one else said anything to you except the woman who was presiding over the coffee table when she informed you that the donuts were only 25 cents each, if you wanted one.

You don't feel that you are a particularly shy person and you certainly don't want to be the focus of a lot of embarrassing attention when you are a first-time visitor in a place, but you wondered after you left that church whether or not you would make the effort to go back there should the occasion arise.

The entire experience was a turn-off.

You also wondered how you would have felt if you were the only white visitor in a congregation of black persons or if you were the only black person visiting in a congregation of only white persons.

What would it take then for you to return?

And yet that church might be the closest one to your place of residence and you would like to be part of your neighborhood church. How long would you tolerate the worship if it seemed unlikely to consider your spiritual needs?

The listening congregation

Just as individual witnesses must first be listeners, so the congregation that is most likely to have an effective witness to people of its neighborhood is the one that listens to what those people have to say about its ministry among them.

Some of the things they might hear are these.

"The sermon has nothing to say to the things that are important to my life."

Another reason, "I can't sing your music and the service is too complicated. I never know where you're at."

"They don't use the Bible in your church."

"I just sit there like I'm watching a show and then I go home. Besides everyone else seems to know every one and they always talk to each other. I don't think anyone knows when I've been there."

"What I need is a job, not prayers!"

Since our church buildings are permitted to occupy space in a particular community by the gracious consent of the people who exempt it from taxation, the congregation would seem to have some obligation to inquire of its neighbors how it can best serve them.

Suppose the people in that neighborhood cannot read English and, in fact, may not be able to read at all. Having a church service which is dependent on the worshipers being able to read a bulletin or follow a long printed liturgical service may make it virtually impossible for them to be part of that *koinonia.*

Or suppose that most of the people drive into the city from affluent suburbs because they want to keep going to the old church of their childhood. They dress well and have no contact with the current church neighbors who may be poor people with different needs than theirs. The political and economic realities of that community are of no interest to those members who come there from other areas.

Reluctant evangelists

To compensate for all of these obstacles to fellowship, members of a congregation have to go out of their way to make the strangers among them feel welcome.

Unfortunately this does not happen very often. More likely, visitors who are "different" feel very unwanted.

If they dress differently or speak with different accents, members either stare silently or avoid eye contact with them.

If they do persist in coming and start to bring with them more people like themselves, the traditional members often exhibit a growing antagonism.

Church members will often profess an interest in evangelism and will even form committees and distribute flyers around the neighborhood inviting people to come to their church but if, by some miracle of the Holy Spirit, new people respond to their invitation in any significant number, the members become quite nervous.

"Will these new people expect us to change the way we've always done things?" they ask each other.

Growing cities, shrinking churches

In the cities of our own country, the situation is desperate as the historic churches abandon the inner city.

Like the people from Cyprus and Cyrene who came to Antioch, we have to start being aggressive in inviting newcomers in our neighborhoods, who are not traditionally the same as "us," to become part of our fellowship.

We whose immigrant ancestors were often forced out of their homelands by persecution similar to that of the people around Stephen can understand the desperate needs of newcomers in a strange land.

Wars displace people and they become refugees who must seek a new life in another country. Famine and poverty force people to flee to new places where there is food and opportunity.

If these newcomers are already Christians they must look to an existing congregation in their neighborhood for a welcome. If they are not Christians, they have even more need for a loving, caring fellowship. The longing and the need for hospitality is intensified by their isolation from their former relationships.

The strangers to our cities also come from other parts of our own country. They often are the children of rural people who have left their home community to seek their fortunes and futures in the great cities. There they often become prey to a variety of tragic possibilities without the aggressive intervention of the church.

Yet the urbanization of our country moves on inexorably, forcing cities to absorb vast numbers of dispossessed people, families, young people, and elderly people—crowding them into old buildings and deteriorating neighborhoods. A few, who make it rich in the cities, isolate themselves in high-rise security buildings where they "cocoon" themselves in splendid independence from the church.

How do we minister effectively to all of these people?

The sacrifice of change

Some things may have to change, and change means sacrifice.

When one changes, one gives up something for the sake of something new.

Most of us resist changing because it involves the pain of loss. We want to hang on to the familiar and the comfortable.

Some people say about their church and its traditional ways of doing things, "We'd rather die than change!"

And, of course, that's what's happening.

Wisdom is required to know what must change and what ought not change.

Our experience with congregations is that the most common reaction to declining numbers is an attempt to revive those programs that worked in the past. But how can one revive a Sunday school when the membership is too old to have children? How does one reorganize a youth program when all of the young people have left the church?

While we're waiting for "the good old days" to come back, all of our energies are flowing backward to the past instead of forward to the future.

Remember those 430-year-old bones of Joseph that the Israelites carried around in the wilderness for 40 years waiting to bury them in the promised land? Too many congregations are carrying around the old bones of the past because they don't know what to do with them as they wander in the wilderness of their present situation.

We tend to glorify the memories of the past. The old bones of tradition never get buried. And some of them should.

Some of the "old bones" of tradition that may need burial are complicated worship forms. Liturgies, litanies, and printed prayers that only seminary-trained clergy are able to handle and music that only professional musicians can perform do not help the neighborhood congregation win people to Jesus Christ!

Not only young people and strangers to the church feel this way but older adults seem to harbor these thoughts also.

Paul Johnson, a Lutheran sociologist, reported on a study of adult Lutherans in which 2000 lay persons and over 700 clergy volunteered their views on worship. Most of them focused on their own worship experiences.

"Seventy-four percent of the clergy," wrote Dr. Johnson, "and 68% of the laity described Lutheran worship services as rigid, boring, too formal, repetitious and bound by tradition" (*The Christian Century,* July 29–August 5, 1987, 656-659).

Is it time to change?

The study Dr. Johnson cited may indicate that changing the liturgy may not be a "sacrifice" at all for most Lutherans!

Church bodies with elaborate liturgical forms, vestments, and processions are not growing, Johnson says.

Churches that win people are those in which familiar, easy-to-sing hymns are sung, prayers are spontaneous, personal, and prayed by both clergy and lay persons, and the messages are biblical and practical. Choirs invite people to sing music within the technical ability of the average person.

Most important, newcomers will not be embarrassed by a worship service that they are unable to sing or understand and that demands previous knowledge of the liturgy.

Of course some churches grow without changing any of the above simply because they are in fast-growing communities, usually in the suburbs where the primary concern of educated, upwardly mobile middle-class families are for programs for their children.

Meeting the needs of people

So we know how to program to meet the needs of upwardly mobile young families. We've been doing that for a long time.

Parents get involved because they know that someone must carry out the programs in which they want their children. For that reason we organize preschools and day-care centers where children can safely grow in a loving environment.

We organize and promote parent education classes and forums on the how-tos of dealing with the developmental problems of every stage of growth. Marriage enrichment programs do well because of the stresses faced by young families in the higher income brackets.

When the young couples grow older and their children move away and the neighborhood stops growing, that's when the church must go to work to redefine its ministry and to determine what the spiritual, social, physical, and psychological needs are in the new-old neighborhood. Unfortunately, that's also the time when the age level of the membership goes up, the energy level drops, and leadership for all programs becomes more difficult to recruit.

Moving on out

The basic human needs for love and belonging, for fellowship and meaning, are still out there beyond the walls of the church.

Instead of the needs of families, the needs may be those of single adults or of one-parent families.

Pastor and people must be united in their commitment to make their church building available as a community center for *all* of the people who live around their building.

Now is the time to start listening to those people.

The pastor cannot simply sit in the office but must get around and show some interest in the church neighbors.

One pastor decided to have her morning coffee at the local cafe rather than in her office. In that way she became visible and available to the people of her community in Chicago.

The remnant people of the congregation cannot just take refuge in past congregational glories. They, if they live near their church, need to become friends of their new neighbors.

Their listening begins as they look for answers to questions that will help them understand the new neighbors better.

"What is life like for these newcomers? What are their pains and their dreams? What can our church do, what does it have to become, to befriend them?"

The witness of the church is always holistic. People are not just souls. They are bodies and minds; they are social and spiritual beings.

When ordinary Christians become interested in "whole" persons, their style of witnessing changes. No longer do they think only of getting members to fill up their pews on Sunday but they become interested in the whole Monday to Saturday life of the people to whom they are led to speak and minister to in the name of Jesus Christ.

You leave your church with joy

Your friend had come to church with you and you were anxious about how things would go. But when you and your friend leave the church that morning, your heart is full of gratitude for the *koinonia* of which you are a part!

Many of the other members stopped to talk to your guest, often ending their brief, but genuinely interested, conversations with their own warm invitations to come back. One family invited both of you to go to brunch with them! You declined, feeling that might be too much for a first visit, but you were grateful.

Most of all you were grateful for an inclusive service and the fact that, this morning, the hymns were familiar and singable and a pianist played a supportive accompaniment to the organ.

The pastor was having a series of Bible study sermons so had cut most of the responses out of the liturgy in order to have time for participation in the study. That Sunday you noticed how many of the other members had brought their own Bibles. Since you had forgotten yours, you shared one of the Bibles from the pew with your friend.

That really worked out to your advantage because you became aware that your visitor did not have much Bible background. Through the participation and feedback from the congregation (into which even your friend entered), the study took on a great deal of relevance to current life situations. The pastor added historical and cultural material that enriched the study and provided fresh theological insights that you had not known before even though the biblical material was a well-known, familiar text.

You explained to your friend that the services were not always like this but that services varied because lay people were part of the preparation of all events in the life of the church. Their ideas and insights, you whispered to your guest, were considered invaluable by your pastor.

When you introduced the pastor to your friend, you all sat down together and talked for a few minutes. During that time, the pastor listened intently to the answers your friend gave to questions. To your delight, your visitor invited the pastor to come over that week to see some special coins from an inherited collection!

Long after you had taken your friend home you found yourself thanking God for the opportunity that had been given to you to be part of another person's spiritual journey. It had taken many weeks, more time than you felt you had at the time, lots of listening, visiting, and caring, but now you knew that you had gained more than you had given.

8

IMITATORS
OF CHRIST

We were going to meet with a "base community"!

As language students in the Mexican city of Cuernavaca, we had been hearing about these gatherings of Catholic lay persons throughout Latin America.

It was exciting, we felt, the way these home Bible study groups were changing the life of the church and the politics of their countries.

The one we were invited to attend met at the small, tin-roofed adobe home of Marcella and her 100-year-old father Pedro. Every week the group gathered to share the study of God's Word, looking up verses, sharing experiences, applying the message to their lives as nonprofessional working people whose opportunities for education and income were limited.

What they explored was the "good news to the poor" that Jesus had come preaching (Luke 4:18). Studying it themselves was like finding treasure in a field hidden from them, in many cases, by their own inability to read and by the neglect of their church to proclaim it to them.

The excitement was contagious as they shared treasure after treasure from the Bible as the Spirit led them in their search. Every sharing was received with thanksgiving sobered only when they began to ponder how they could put the "good news" to practice in their individual and corporate lives.

Unlike most Bible study groups in our country, these groups do not look for theological abstractions but for what the Bible has to say about the real issues and problems in their barrios and the political realities of their country and city. In one evening the discussion might focus on clean water (or in some places on available water), on health issues, on the removal of a sympathetic bishop and his replacement with a conservative cleric, or on the work of a "cooperative" in that area.

All of this was done in the context of the gospel and prayer.

Although many North Americans have never heard about base communities (communidades de base), there are thousands of them even among students and middle class people, but most are among the poor, in slums, in squatters' settlements and campesinos in the rural areas.

Like the man in Chapter 8 of Luke, they "tell all over town" how much Jesus is doing for them! As a result people are drawn to their message and new base communities keep springing up.

Renewal in the church

The history of the church reveals that the church begins to bubble with new life whenever ordinary people are "joined together constantly in prayer" (Acts

1:14), and start taking seriously the promise of Jesus that the Spirit would come with power to make them witnesses in Jerusalem, Judea, Samaria, Cuernavaca, and your home town.

In the 17th century, Lutheranism in Germany was stultified by scholasticism and the substitution of fixed, dogmatic interpretation of the Scriptures for a vital relationship between the believer and God.

Lay people were forced into a passive role, recipients of the teachings of the church, expected only to attend, take the sacrament, listen to pulpit preaching, and observe church rules.

But no matter how seemingly dead the church becomes, the Holy Spirit works to bring about the renewal of its life.

A 17th century German pastor named Philipp Jakob Spener was inspired to gather a little group of praying people in his home for Bible study and the discussion of the Sunday sermons. The aim was to deepen the spiritual life of the people.

Soon these "circles" were meeting in many homes and Spener put forth the almost forgotten Lutheran conviction that all believers are priests and proposed that all congregations should gather these *ecclesiolae in ecclesia* (little churches in the church) for mutual helpfulness and growth in the Christian life.

Naturally, just as the base communities have come under the criticism of the church hierarchy in Latin America, so did the movement started by Spener. While it's true that some of Spener's followers became excessively strict, as a whole the movement was of great value for the religious life of Germany and the renewal of the Lutheran church, saving it from the dead orthodoxy into which it was in danger of falling.

When the Anglican clergyman John Wesley realized that the life of his church body needed reviving, he came to the conclusion that large evangelistic meetings could only take people so far in their search for new life. Eventually he was convinced that they had to be gathered in small groups around Bible study and prayer.

His own transforming experience came at an Anglican small group "society" meeting when the leader was reading from Luther's preface to the *Commentary on Romans*.

When he was no longer allowed to preach in Anglican pulpits, and not wanting to start "churches," he formed his own societies, later dividing them into "classes" of 12 members with a lay leader. As a result of these small Methodist groups, the life of the Protestant churches in both England and America was renewed.

Isn't that the way the New Testament church grew?

The "church in the house" was a necessity and a blessing in the missionary outreach of the early church. Paul sent greetings to his friends Prisca and Aquila and also to "the church that meets at their house" (Rom. 16:3-5).

He sent greetings to the believers at Laodicea, and to Nympha and the church in her house" (Col. 4:15). We will never know how many of these house churches became the seeds from which the Christian church grew into a universal fellowship.

Once a week is not enough

If the church is to make any lasting witness to the world it must be more than a "Sunday church." The real witness of the church is made through the Monday-to-Saturday life of its members.

The way to keep that witness alive is to fellowship with other Christians around the Bible at least once a week between Sundays. The "church in the house" or the *"ecclesiolae in ecclesia"* may be the most effective way of making this a reality.

Such groups also become a less threatening environment into which to bring people who are not used to going to church. Who can object to receiving an invitation to a gathering in someone's home? When lay people are the leaders of these groups, the threat is further reduced. No authority figure is there to be impressed or satisfied with "right" answers.

The wise pastor will, of course, know what is going on in the groups, keep in touch with the leaders, talk with them about their understandings of biblical texts, and offer them resource materials. At the same time the pastor does not try to control the groups but trusts the Spirit to work through the Word to bring new life (and maybe some new directions?) to the church fellowship.

In addition, then, to the usual women's circles, men's breakfast fellowships and youth groups, we need both sexes in groups which are cross-cultural and cross-generational.

The imitators

The apostle Paul seemed to think that the best way to witness was by being an "imitator of Christ." He even urged people to imitate Paul himself since he was an imitator of Christ. "Imitate me, then," he wrote to the Corinthian church, "just as I imitate Christ" (1 Cor. 11:1 TEV).

Do you see why we need to stay close to the life, teachings, and actions of Jesus?

As we gather around the Word, the Holy Spirit will reshape us into the image of the Christ of the Bible.

A young boy is said to have asked an artist how he was able to chisel an angel out of a block of stone.

The artist replied, "First I saw the angel in my heart. Then I saw it in the stone and released it."

As we grow closer to Jesus Christ through the Word, the Spirit chisels out of our spirits the shape of Jesus. We assume his likeness and find ourselves acting as he acted.

If our churches are undergoing a moral crisis, it's because, as Ralph Waldo Emerson once said, "What we are speaks so loud that they can't hear what we say."

In the small groups of gathered Christians, we can serve as correctives to one another, "speaking the truth in love" so that we can "in all things grow up into him who is the Head, that is, Christ" (Eph. 4:15).

Jesus' first and last words to his disciples were, and are, "Follow me!" When he has touched our lives, that contact becomes our call to discipleship.

Mark's gospel tells the marvelous story of a blind man named Bartimaeus, who was sitting by the roadside, begging.

Jesus came by. That beggar had heard of him and when he came near, the blind man called out for mercy and for sight.

When Jesus spoke the words of healing, we are told that "immediately he received his sight and *followed Jesus along the road*" (Mark 10:46-52—italics ours).

The life goal of the newly-sighted man from that point on was to become an "imitator of Jesus" who had revealed himself to him through his healing action.

The kind of scandalous behavior that makes a mockery of Jesus will only alienate the world from the church.

When religious leaders and evangelists are held up to public view as persons who live lavish life-styles with descriptions of luxurious mansions and closets full of expensive clothing, even the least informed person recognizes that their lives are a contradiction to the life of the one who said that he did not even have a place to lay his head (Matt. 8:20).

When religious people claw and bite at each other in public disputes, they become a contradiction of the Bible's teaching that we who profess the name of Christ, "be kind and compassionate to one another, forgiving each other, just as in Christ God forgave you" (Eph. 4:32).

The Christian's behavior is to demonstrate that we are "imitators of God," and "dearly loved children" (Eph. 5:1).

Every quarrel between Christians, every schism in the church, every scandal that the individual follower of Christ is involved in, reflects to the world a Christ whom, they assume, is the author of such behavior.

During the height of the publicity over a sex scandal involving television evangelists Jim and Tammy Bakker, a church convention was being held at a large hotel near the Los Angeles airport. One of the speakers was on the elevator going down to breakfast on the first floor, passing the second floor where a convention business meeting was already in progress. One of the other hotel guests, not a part of the convention, said, as the elevator went past the second floor, "So you're not going to the 'Tammy party' either?"

As the speaker recounted the episode to the convention in his next speech, he commented, "Whenever anything happens anywhere in the body of Christ, we are all tarred with the same brush."

Most of all, the name of Christ is tarred.

Witnessing by imitation of Christ

The church must have leaders who imitate Christ so that the rest of us can imitate them!

The people of Thessalonica "turned to God from idols to serve the living and true God," because they saw how Paul and Silas and Timothy lived among them (1 Thess. 1:5).

As a result, the Thessalonians who had received their witness to the gospel "not simply with words," but "with power, with the Holy Spirit" in turn "became imitators" not only of those witnesses but also "of the Lord!"

And the witness by imitation went on.

The Thessalonians "became a model to all the believers in Macedonia and in Achaia." The Lord's message, wrote Paul, "rang out from you not only in Macedonia and Achaia—your faith in God has become known everywhere" (1 Thess. 1:4-8).

Do you see? While words are necessary at times, the power of a life lived in imitation of Christ gives that word credibility and power in the world.

Your witness must include with absolute conviction the injunction to others to "imitate me, then, just as I imitate Christ."

A pastor who does not model what she or he preaches to others will not inspire others to live as imitators of Christ. If the leaders of the church never witness to others of their faith in Christ, what example will the people have to imitate?

If the leadership of the church lives a life-style that does not reflect the simple, other-centered style of Jesus, what right have they to demand sacrificial giving of the time, energy, and money of the people who are asked by the Word to be imitators of them?

When pastor and people are united in a whole-hearted desire to "run straight toward the goal in order to win the prize, which is God's call through Christ Jesus to the life above," then they have a right to urge each other to "keep on imitating me" and "pay attention to those who follow the right example we have set for you" (Phil. 3:14, 17 TEV).

Like Paul we can only look "with tears" on those who "live as enemies of the cross of Christ." They are those whose "god is their stomach" whose "glory is in their shame," whose minds are "on earthly things" (Phil. 3:18-19).

Don't wait to be perfect

If Paul had waited to be a perfect person before he went about testifying to what Jesus had done for him and asking people to imitate him, we would not have his letters to read today!

Paul quarreled with Peter (Gal. 2:11). He argued with Barnabas about taking Mark with them on their second missionary journey because Mark had left them on the first journey. As a result of the argument the team of Barnabas and Paul split, each one of them going his own way with a new partner (Acts 15:36-40).

In his letter to the Philippians, Paul confessed that he had not yet obtained his goal of becoming like Jesus or of having "already been made perfect" but, he said, "I press on." That pressing on means that we forgive our past mistakes and strain "toward what is ahead" (Phil. 3:12-13).

With this as his confession, Paul could still say "keep on imitating me."

With all of our "warts," we are all we have to give to others.

So we press on.

Part of Paul's pressing on included being reconciled with Mark so that at the end of his life he could write to the Colossians from prison about Mark who was with him, that "if he comes to you, welcome him" (Col. 4:10).

Be kind and compassionate to one another. . . .

We sin and are sinned against. We keep on forgiving and being forgiven.

Forgiveness is the heart of the gospel, a norm for the kingdom of God, and it's in our forgiving that we become imitators of Christ.

We gather to scatter

The base communities, the Methodist societies and classes, the *ecclesiolae in ecclesia,* and all of our Bible circles, never exist as an end in themselves.

We gather in order to receive inspiration and instruction for our scattering. It's out there, in the world, that we are to be imitators of Christ, healing, teaching, proclaiming, demonstrating what the love of God is all about.

No matter how many small groups meet and enjoy their meetings, unless the people get out of their groups and into the neighborhood where they can listen and respond to the needs of the people, their church will not be worth imitating.

Jesus was always out among the people.

As imitators of him, that's where we will be.

Pastor Carl Brown shepherds Valley Queen Church, an American Baptist congregation in one of the poorest areas in the United States, a congregation that has been cited by the Ford Foundation as a "model church."

Pastor Brown says that "there is a desperate need

to incorporate together the spiritual and political sides" of our daily lives. Sounds like the base communities, doesn't it?

"Churches," he reflects, "have allowed themselves to grow apart from the concerns of the people. . . . There was a time when I didn't encourage people outside of the church. Yet now I see that when people have no shoes, how can you bring them back unless you meet those needs?"

He concludes, "You either bring them out or you go to them. . . . How can you tell them about a Jesus they can't see or feel?"

In order for the people of their community to believe in Jesus, the congregation sends them people they can see and feel.

Valley Queen Church has "conducted workshops on health care, crime prevention, the electoral process, job training and placement, continuing adult education, legislative and administrative advocacy, and many others."

Because the "causes of community problems are deep and complex" the church organized the Valley Queen Community Outreach and Housing Development Corporation, Inc., a corporation that "functions on a daily basis: planning, organizing, implementing activities, approaches, programs, and projects to uplift and motivate the inhabitants."

The church did this, said the pastor, because "Sunday worship, Bible classes, and church fellowship could not alone fill the gap."

Pastor Brown warns that the "church should not be a threat to the community. . . . For instance, we should be careful not to allow professionalism to block out the spirit of Christ. We want that spirit to show through us." (*Grapevine*, vol. 18 no. 9, April 1987).

Imitators of Christ.

Be out among the people

Valley Queen Church knows what are the needs of its neighbors, even up to 20 miles away. The members of the base communities are concerned about the whole life of their world. Ministry in both places is to the whole person, just as was the ministry of Jesus.

Affirming that the whole person includes both body and spirit, Jesus could say to the paralyzed man, "Son, your sins are forgiven," and then add, "Get up, take your mat and walk." When questioned, he simply explained, "Which is easier: to say to the paralytic, 'Your sins are forgiven,' or to say, 'Get up, take your mat and walk'?" (Mark 2:5-12).

Both commands speak to the needs of a whole person.

Because ministry must always be to the whole person, the congregation must be involved with the whole life of the people it serves.

If they are "yuppies," what are their lives like? Where are their hurts, their needs?

If they are elderly and on fixed incomes, what bothers them?

If they are single parents, how can they be sustained in the stresses of their lives?

If they are refugees who have lost their home and all of their relationships, what can we do to supply their needs?

How do we become imitators of Christ to them all?

In Latin America, they gather in their base communities to find out from the Bible what Jesus and his followers did that turned their world upside down. They help each other to understand how that message can apply to them and what they do.

Then they go out and do it.

And these ordinary Christians are changing their world.

9

BEARERS OF HOPE

G*od rules!*

A bumper sticker bearing that triumphant announcement was on a car parked outside the dormitory at the university.

Actually, the task of the Messiah was to make that announcement.

"The time has come," Jesus announced, "The kingdom of God is near. Repent and believe the good news!"

Later, he sent the 12 apostles out to "preach the kingdom of God and to heal" and they went "from village to village preaching the gospel and healing people everywhere" because the gospel and the kingdom were one and the same thing (Luke 9:1-6).

The same assignment was given to 70 others who were sent out two by two to "heal the sick" and to announce "the kingdom of God is near you" (Luke 10:1-9).

The world is ready for newness

Is God in charge?

That's not the news we're getting today, is it?

War in the Middle East with the Persian Gulf erupting in oily flames!

Planes near-missing each other and not missing each other in the skies over most cities.

Violent outbursts and shootings on the highways!

The macabre stockpiling of frightfully expensive and awesomely destructive nuclear weapons while millions go hungry!

Incest, rape, and the abuse and exploitation of children!

Middle-class adolescents killing themselves by the hundreds!

Drunken drivers slaughtering each other and others on the highways!

What would you like to add to the list?

Birth control by abortion? The exploitation of women and racial minorities by employers? Unemployment? Increasing poverty of the already poor? Growing homelessness?

Is God in charge? Does God *rule*?

Never have we been more ready to hear the good news of the kingdom! "The kingdom of God is near!"

It's already here but not yet complete.

"God rules" is the theme of the last book of the Bible. The promise of the Revelation is that the day is coming when Jesus will return to judge the nations. At that time there will be "a new heaven and a new earth" and God will be "making everything new" (Rev. 21:1-5). But we don't have to wait. The kingdom, the reign of God, is here now! It was ushered in by Jesus Christ, the promised Messiah.

He announced it and he will return to this earth to consummate it. For the present, we work, we witness, and we wait.

God rules.

The reign of God and the church

You may have heard this saying: "Jesus preached the kingdom but what we got was the church!"

Depending on one's point of view or past experience that statement is quoted with bitter irony or with jubilation.

Perhaps the phrase *"koinonia* becoming kingdom" might be a better description of the relationship of the church to the kingdom of God.

Our fellowship, our sharing, our lives together in the church are to be a demonstration of the "rule of God," an example on this earth of the kingdom which is now and which is also to come.

If the church is to model in the present what the kingdom is to be in its ultimate glory then the task is one in which all of us who have been baptized into Christ must be engaged.

At Christmas many parents are struck with the problem of trying to teach their children the meaning of Christmas in the midst of contrary messages. Children recite their lists of Christmas wants to a department store Santa for army fatigues, laser death rays, and "masheen guns" while strains of "Silent Night" play in the background: "Sleep in heavenly peace."

Perhaps this is the reason someone suggested that Christians ought to do their daily prayers with the Bible in one hand and the newspaper in the other. The daily news keeps our feet firmly on earth when there is danger of our head being too other-worldly.

No one of us can sit comfortably in our pew when we are faced daily with the enormity of the unfinished task for the church.

At the same time, we can leave the pew with the sure and certain conviction that the gospel is the bearer of hope in the midst of the hopelessness of most of the world's news.

The same newspapers, however, which keep us re-minded of the reasons why our witness to the gospel is urgent also brief us with accounts of the gospel's power to make a difference.

A story in the *Los Angeles Times* (Aug. 17, 1987) was both heartbreaking and heartwarming, just like the grace of God.

Three mornings a week, wrote Robert S. Weiss, a *Times* staff writer, an air-conditioned bus drives into "Tent City," L.A.'s urban campground for 600 homeless people.

Most of the 75 children who live in the dusty tents run toward the bus yelling, "It's here! It's here!"

The bus is the good news for children who live in the fearful environment of Tent City without privacy, without enough food, and with the constant threat of assault.

Operated by a skid row mission run by Fred Jordan and his wife Willie, the bus gives the children of Tent City a chance "to be young," to be in a place that's free of glass, insects, the smell of urine, and the threat of bodily harm.

They are given food, private showers, toys, shoes, wholesome love and evidence of a reality other than Tent City.

The reporter quoted Walter Contreras, the mission's day camp director, as saying, "I feel that I bring the kids some hope. That's what drives me along each day. I pray that each day we're a little bit closer to a future. Oh, if I only had money. These kids need so much."

I bring the kids some hope. . . .

Each day a little bit closer to a future. . . .

Evidence of a reality other than Tent City. . . .

What they are doing and describing is the kingdom of God. Were it not for the promise of the coming kingdom there would be no hope, no future to look forward to.

What the Jordans and Contreras are doing now brings the future closer. They are signs of the kingdom, marks of a church living now in the realm of God.

The excitement of being the kingdom

The kingdom of God is living and active! It generates its own energy and its own excitement.

Those who dare to enter into its life will be awed by the fact that they share in a reality that has power to transform, heal, change, bring peace, delight, give meaning, and to save.

The fact that the church is here to witness to the kingdom makes it more than an organization or an institution. With the cross at the center of its life as evidence to the fact that the kingdom has come, the church is a magnet that has the power to draw people to it.

In the middle of many of the towns in England we saw a statue of the person whom the townspeople felt was responsible for giving life to that place. The city was marked by that presence and the remembered deeds of the sculpted one.

The congregation that lives in the reign of God looks to the one at the center of its life for its mission and purpose.

Perhaps one of the debilitating slogans which many of us have been guilty of promoting, often with good intentions, voices the idea that "being is more important than doing."

But the book of Acts begins by telling us that, as a sequel to the gospel according to Luke, it is the record of all that "Jesus began to do and to teach" (1:1).

What we *do* shapes what we are.

The congregation that is *doing* the things of the kingdom will draw people into its fellowship because they will see it *being* the kingdom.

Its members will not have to work so hard organizing evangelism committees and worrying about what to say in order to be witnesses. They will be too busy witnessing by their response to the hurts and the ills of the world around them.

When you read the story of the Tent City children, don't you feel drawn to that operation?

Why did we see so many young people in Africa who had come there to work with the Peace Corps and with the mission stations? Why did they go there to live with snakes, termites, torrid heat and torrential rains when they could have stayed in their own developed countries and lived in comfort?

Besides the fact that they found love and acceptance from the African people, they were obviously drawn there by the knowledge that a life given in response to the needs of others is a life worth living.

Similarly, when people hear about a congregation that lives as though it were part of the present and coming reign of God they get excited and want to be part of that resurrected life energy.

Marks of the kingdom

The apostle Paul has given us some "marks" of the kingdom. In Romans 14:17, he wrote that the kingdom of God is "righteousness, peace and joy in the Holy

Spirit. . . . Let us therefore make every effort to do what leads to peace and mutual edification."

Do what leads to peace.

If peace is one of the marks of the reign of God, then never has the church needed to play the role of the peacemaker any more than it does now.

The promised kingdom was to be the bearer of *shalom*, a Hebrew word that means wholeness, peace, health, and prosperity for all, not just for a few.

The Messiah was to be called the "prince of peace." Peace with God was his first gift, then peace with other humans. The veil that divided priest from people in the Temple was torn in two at his death and all the walls of hostility came tumbling down when the cross claimed his life. "He came and preached peace to you who were far away and peace to those who were near" (Eph. 2:17).

The primary message of the kingdom is peace. The church torn by controversy and divisions, the congregation that denies access to some groups of people, repels people and destroys its witness to the *shalom* of the kingdom.

The congregation marked by the kingdom's call to peace will not engage in nor support any rhetoric that promotes the need of their nation to be first or number one in the world. Rather it will underscore the warning of Jesus that "many who are first will be last, and many who are last will be first" (Matt. 19:30).

Imagine what a change the church could make in the world's peace causes if all of the Christians insisted that peacemaking was their kingdom priority. With the money spent now on arms, all the hungry of the world would have food to eat, the homeless would have shelter, and everyone in the world could drink pure water!

That's the kind of hope the kingdom stirs up because the promise is that God

> will judge between the nations
>> and will settle disputes for many peoples.
> They will beat their swords into plowshares,
>> and their spears into pruning hooks.
> Nation will not take up sword against nation,
>> nor will they train for war anymore.
>
> (Isa. 2:4)

The cynic will say, "That's wishful thinking."

The Christian says, "That's kingdom thinking and that's why the church keeps praying, 'Your kingdom come, your will be done *on earth* as it is in heaven.' "

Since the kingdom is God's new order we know that "the old" must pass away because "the new" has come. War, so much a part of the old order, and the making of wars must cease when newness comes.

God rules.

Righteousness is also a mark of the kingdom.

Please don't think that God's righteousness means simply being nice people who never get into trouble. The righteousness of the kingdom has little to do with our childhood notions of being good girls and boys.

On the contrary, Jesus said that the righteousness of the kingdom surpasses that of the Pharisees and the teachers of the law (Matt. 5:20). It does not concern itself with rule-keeping or with going public with one's prayers or charities.

The kingdom demands a righteousness so profound that no one has ever lived up to its requirements. Which one of us can always love our enemies, never look lustfully at another, never be angry, not lay up treasures on earth, and not worry about tomorrow?

Our righteousness is only possible because we are clothed in the righteousness of our Lord Jesus Christ and we are "found in him" (Phil. 3:9).

When we entrust our lives to him, then we have the same mind that was in Christ, so that we think his thoughts and do his works. We become imitators of Christ.

Then we understand that righteousness, in kingdom terms, is radically different from the works-righteousness preached by so many.

Now we begin to comprehend why the prophets always associated "righteousness" with "justice," and not with worship or offerings but with concern for the widow and the orphan and the refugee or migrant. Listen to the prophet Amos:

> I hate, I despise your religious feasts;
>   I cannot stand your assemblies.
> Even though you bring me burnt offerings and grain
>   offerings,
> I will not accept them.
> Though you bring choice fellowship offerings
> I will have no regard for them.
> Away with the noise of your songs!
>   I will not listen to the music of your harps.
> But let justice roll on like a river,
>   righteousness like a never-failing stream!
>   (Amos 5:21-24)

Righteousness and justice are twin concepts to Amos.

The easy way of keeping rules and living a Sunday religion is not the way of the kingdom. The Lord of the kingdom warns us to "beware of the teachers of the law. They like to walk around in flowing robes and love to be greeted in the marketplaces and have the most important seats in the synagogues and the places of honor at banquets. They devour widows' houses and for a show make lengthy prayers" (Luke 20:45-47).

When one is absorbed in seeing that justice is done to the poor, the abused, the victimized, the sinned-against of society, that, according to Luke, is piety.

Our needs for love, for belonging, for meaning, and for excitement which may once have driven us to find satisfaction in adulteries, alcohol, drugs, or violence are now satisfied by our involvements in the demands for justice for the poor and the oppressed.

The Christian church is still the foremost champion of human rights and individual dignity.

It's *koinonia* becoming kingdom.

Walking into the future with joy

Righteousness, peace and joy in the Holy Spirit. . . .

The light of the coming reign of God is the beacon leading us into God's future and brightening the path we now walk.

Now we begin to see our witnessing and our invitation to our neighbors to come to church in a new light—the light of the kingdom of God. We are not inviting people only to meetings, or services, or to small group meetings, but when we invite them to be "converted," to be baptized and to join the church, we are really calling them to participate in the kingdom of God!

We are confronting them with the possibility of a transformed world, with the radical relationship of the kingdom, with becoming peacemakers, with doing justice, and we are calling them to follow a king who reigns from a cross!

We're going to be "as shrewd as snakes and as innocent as doves" because the proclamation of the kingdom sends us out "like sheep among wolves" (Matt. 10:16), perhaps to be torn to shreds.

We will leave to God the result of our proclamation and our doing of the kingdom to God. All that's required of us is that we be faithful to our vocation as witnesses to God's reign in Christ. You may start on your witnessing journey with fear and lack of confidence. But remember the 72 who were sent out to announce the kingdom. They "returned with joy and said, 'Lord, even the demons submit to us in your name.' " (Luke 10:17).

You may feel more like a timid child than a bold herald of the kingdom, but as you encounter seekers along the way and share your good news with them you will become more and more aware that you are not on the journey alone. All the time that you were reaching out, touching, speaking, doing, the Spirit of Jesus was leading you, going before you, putting in your way those whose lives needed what you have to give.

And you will return with joy, amazed at the demons that were subject to you in the name of Jesus!

People whose relationships had turned sour learned to love one another again. Adults who had been abused as children experienced healing of their soiled memories. Angry skeptics began to doubt their own doubts and the rejected ones lost their bitterness in the floodtide of their own forgiveness.

"For the kingdom of God is not a matter of words but of power" (1 Cor. 4:20) and when you go in the name of the one who brings the reign of God with him, you will see that power at work even through your witness.

Then you will know that "the kingdom of the world has become the kingdom of our Lord" (Rev. 11:15).

Hastening the Day

Perhaps all of this chapter must be one of the "secrets" of the kingdom when we go about our witness.

Do you think your friend who accepts your invitation to come to church could stand knowing all that his or her acceptance of your invitation might mean?

Probably not.

So we will listen and witness and invite and we will leave the rest to God. It's the task of God's Spirit to call and gather believers into the kingdom. We simply issue the invitation and bring them into the fellowship, the *koinonia*.

If the church is "the *koinonia* becoming kingdom" then the kingdom is on its way.

By our testimony we can hasten that day. Jesus promised that "this gospel of the kingdom will be preached in the whole world as a testimony to all nations and then the end will come" (Matt. 24:14).

10

LIVING ON THE EDGE

God is calling us to live on the edges of life, where newness comes. The horizon is both the place where day breaks and where it finally yields to night.

The edges of the gospel and the church are flexible, permeable, and open to newness.

Jesus calls people to leave the safe centers of existence and to move toward the edges. "Go out to the roads and country lanes," he commands in one of his parables, "and make them come in, so that my house will be full" (Luke 14:23).

Danger lurks in the country lanes and rides on the roads but people are there and opportunity waits. Out there those with hunger for God and thirst for the water of life respond to those who come with an invitation to a banquet.

We don't have to provide the banquet. God has already spread the table. All we have to do is to invite people to the feast.

Preparing for the journey

The distance from safe center to the edge may be a long, long journey. How many years has it been since you found that secure place for your own life?

Are you ready to go back out?

Someone left their place of safety to find you. Are you ready to do that for someone else?

We ordinary Christians are not asked to preach to the multitudes or to evangelize the crowds. Our great calling is to go out into the streets and lanes of our cities and towns and to invite individuals, one at a time.

Focus on that task.

Begin today.

Find a place where you can be quiet. Combine it with a time of stillness. Five or ten minutes will do nicely.

Enter into that time and that place. Sit on a not-too-comfortable chair, feet firmly on the floor, hands on your lap, palms up, waiting.

Focus on the Spirit of Jesus within you (1 Cor. 3:16; Acts 16:7). Just as the Spirit led the apostle Paul by a vision to witness to a woman named Lydia in a town called Philippi, so you can be sure that the Spirit who empowers all of our witnessing will lead you to the one who is waiting for your witness.

Discipline yourself to focus, expectantly, for as many days as it takes to get ready to move out into your roads and country lanes or into your Macedonia. You will become aware of a gathering and growing excitement in your spiritual life as you wait.

What can you expect? Look for a face or a place to take shape in your spirit's eye. The place might be the aisle of a food market, or the playgound where you take your children to play, or the gym where you work out, or the table where you sit for coffee at the office, or the route where you walk every morning.

Only God knows the place, the person, and the time.

The person will be there waiting.

You might be surprised. It may be someone you know well or someone you've never met before.

The apostle Paul was surprised when he got to Macedonia.

The vision he received from the Spirit was of a man of Macedonia who was "standing and begging him 'Come over to Macedonia and help us' " (Acts 16:9).

But when Paul got there, instead of a man, there was a woman named Lydia waiting. Paul, as a Pharisee of the "strictest sect" (Acts 26:5), was not even supposed to speak to a woman in public, not even his female relatives.

Because Paul was willing to leave the safe center of his existence and talk to one who was on the edges of the religious life of his world, another whole continent was opened to the gospel. Lydia's heart was opened to "respond to Paul's message" (16:14).

As a result she was baptized along with her household and she offered Paul and his fellow travelers the hospitality of her house which then became the center for missionary action in the area around Philippi.

So start listening to the Spirit. You will be given one person at a time. Don't run ahead of the Spirit, but don't delay responding either.

Witness at the edges

Experience tells us that renewal of our individual lives and renewal in the church comes from the underside and the edges of life. Out there, among the outcasts and the despised, life can be resurrected.

Who are the outcasts and the despised to you? Don't be surprised if, like Paul, the vision turns out to be someone other than those *you* consider to be worthy of the gospel! Perhaps you already have your "vision" that calls you to the edge of your existence and to the despised ones in your world. Have you answered that call to witness? Is fear holding you back?

Do you know what will happen to you if you meet somebody out at the edges of your existence, someone totally different than the people at your safe center? Out of their sharing of their hearts with you and the sharing of your heart with them, will come spiritual power such as you have never known before!

Jesus was certainly at the edge of his society. He was rejected by people at the center, by the priests and the teachers of the law and the rulers. The political structures plotted his death. His best friends were fishermen, tax collectors, and sinners (Matt. 9:10-11)! Today Jesus would be identified with the homeless, the street people, and be told by the authorities to move on. In fact he was even told by some people in his day to get out of their town (Mark 5:17).

One of the mysteries of our faith is this: God seems to identify most closely with the poor and the despised. Jesus, God's Son, grew up in a town so lowly in the social scale that people asked, when told that he came from Nazareth, "Nazareth! Can anything good come from there?" (John 1:46).

His mother was so poor that she could only afford the most meager of offerings when she went up to the Temple for her ritual purification for childbirth. Because she couldn't afford a lamb, she brought a pair of doves.

So don't be surprised.

Instead, be ready to meet Jesus in disguise, probably in the form of someone who would be the last person in the world to whom you would have decided to witness on your own! But, because you were willing to witness and you sought guidance from the Holy Spirit, you will be given the great opportunity to be renewed in your own Spirit.

The church through the ages has always been renewed by those who chose to be with those at the edges, on the fringes, of society. Francis of Assisi, giving up an inheritance to live among the poor and the lepers; Mother Teresa, living with the diseased and dying of the streets of Calcutta; these people are few in number but mighty in spiritual power.

My own spirit was renewed when I had the privilege of listening to a young man tell of his journey into the valley of death with AIDS. Surely he is among the despised in our country. People with AIDS have been refused places in schools, they have been turned away by medical facilities, their homes have been burned, they have been asked by hosts not to use their toilets, and have been fed on paper plates when others are served on china.

As I listened to him tell of three friends whose funerals he had attended in recent months, of others rejected by their families and friends, and heard him testify to the presence and grace of God that he had experienced through all of these hardships, I felt my own faith being renewed and my heart being filled with compassion for all of the people now suffering with AIDS and for those who will suffer and die in the future.

Did I witness to the young man who spoke? All I could do at the time was to listen and to care. Now I will have to begin the task of facing my own response to the question, "What is my witness now that the Spirit has spoken to me?"

Coping with the requirements of witnessing

Since studies have indicated that most U.S. Christians want their churches to be places of comfort and a retreat from the stresses of every day, how are we going to cope with the requirements of witnessing?

I think that witnessing brings its own renewal. Like Jesus said to his disciples when they returned with food and found him absorbed in conversation with the Samaritan woman, "I have food to eat that you know nothing about" (John 4:32).

When they asked each other, "Could someone have brought him food?" he answered, "My food is to do the will of him who sent me. . . . "

Witnessing is exciting business! It may be one of the few means we have left in our compartmentalized lives for touching the heart of another human being. The need to touch another's life may be behind the rise of popular mysticism and the attempt to communicate with people who lived thousands of years ago in other places. It's so difficult to get close to people in the present, so let's try the past! Fortunes are being made by "channelers" who claim to be able to make these connections. The idea of reincarnation opens up, to seekers for intimacy, worlds of connections in their fantasized other lives.

While witnessing brings its own renewal as Jesus told his disciples, it also forces us back to our faith communities, to our personal devotional life, and to the fellowship of the Word.

There we can tap all of the sources of strength available to the Christian witness. Our friends in the faith will help heal the wounds that come from our encounters at the edge and give us valuable counsel for the continuing excursions into the world of witnessing.

The 72 returned with joy!

If we are serious about the renewal of the body of Christ and the fulfillment of our own discipleship, we will follow the Spirit to the edges and the underside of society.

Jesus is there, waiting for us to recognize him and join him.

He is calling us ordinary Christians to be his witnesses to a new age for the church and for the world.